Life in the UK Test
Study Guide

**The essential study guide
for British citizenship and
settlement tests**

Published by Red Squirrel Publishing

Red Squirrel Publishing
Suite 235, 77 Beak Street,
London, W1F 9DB, United Kingdom

www.redsquirrelbooks.com

First edition published in 2006
Third Edition – Third Impression

Study Guide : ISBN 978-0-9552159-4-0
Study Guide + CD ROM: ISBN 978-0-9552159-6-4

Edited by Henry Dillon, Alastair Smith and Erwan Pirou
Designed and artworked by Cox Design Partnership,
Witney, Oxon
Printed and bound in the United Kingdom

CONTENTS

continued overleaf >

CONTENTS

INTRODUCTION

Choosing to make the United Kingdom your permanent home is an exciting decision made by over 100,000 people every year. However, the decision to seek settlement or to become a British citizen is only the start of what can be a long and challenging journey. The application process is complex, time consuming and expensive.

An important part of the process is the Life in the UK test. The test requires you to learn about life in this country based on information provided by the Home Office. This book is designed to make this stage in the settlement or citizenship process a whole lot easier.

One in three people fail the test. At £34 for every test taken, this is an expensive mistake, and an unnecessary one. By using this book to learn the required material you can walk into your test confident that you will be one of the people who pass the test on their first attempt. And you will be one important step closer to making Britain your home.

About this book

This study guide is intended for people planning to take the Life in the UK Test. It is designed to help you pass the Life in the UK Test first time.

This new edition incorporates revised study materials from the Home Office, which were introduced on 2 April 2007. The revised study materials have greatly expanded the amount of information that must be learnt, making study more challenging. The many features of this book, however, will make your task a lot more straightforward.

It also points you toward the information that is most important and most likely to be included in your test.

The study guide includes various ideas and study methods to help you learn quickly, efficiently and effectively. Choose the ideas and methods that work best for you.

Finally, the guide provides helpful guidance and advice on the settlement and citizenship application processes, and the part that the Life in the UK test plays in both.

Take some time to read through the next section thoroughly. It tells you about all the features of the guide and will enable you to get as much out of it as possible. Check our website **www.lifeintheuk.net** for the latest updates to the book and for extra information about the test.

SEND US YOUR FEEDBACK

Our books have helped thousands of people pass the Life in the UK Test. So we're always delighted when we hear from our readers.

You can send your comments by visiting us at www.lifeintheuk.net/feedback

HOW TO USE THIS STUDY GUIDE

This study guide has many parts and features. But the parts of the book that you must focus on first are the official study materials. These study materials have been reproduced in full from a separate publication from the Home Office called *Life in the United Kingdom: A Journey to Citizenship*. The official study materials start on page 31. You must make sure you read these parts carefully as the questions that you will be asked when you sit your test are all based on these materials.

As you read through the study materials make notes of what you think are the key points.

The other parts of this book support the study materials by making them easier to understand and learn. There are also practice tests that will help you prepare for your test by checking your knowledge.

The study materials are divided into five easy to learn chapters:

● A Changing Society

● UK Today: A Profile

● How the United Kingdom is Governed

● Everyday Needs

● Employment

Chapter Introductions

Each chapter includes an introduction to tell you what to expect and to alert you to the key themes and ideas to look for in the text.

Revision Questions

Revision questions are provided throughout the chapters so that you can check your understanding of the materials as you read them.

Tips and Warnings

There are two symbols used throughout this book.

Read our handy tips for useful advice that could save you a lot of time and effort. We have gathered a lot of useful information since our last edition based on our research and feedback from readers.

Pay close attention to any warnings. They highlight common mistakes that people make when applying for settlement or citizenship. By following our advice you can avoid these mistakes and help your application go smoothly.

Words to Know

The guide also contains an extensive glossary of words that you need to know. These are words or phrases that you will need to understand for your test or are terms that you may need to know to give you background to the official study materials. Each word or phrase is explained fully, in easy to understand language. As you work your way through the materials you can use the Words to Know section to check any terms or expressions that are not familiar.

Practice Questions

Once you've finished revising the study materials, try answering the practice questions. These questions are arranged in ten practice tests; each test contains 24 questions. This is exactly the same format as the official test. Use the tear out marking sheet on page 203 for easy marking.

ABOUT THE TEST

The Life in the UK Test was first introduced in November 2005 as a requirement for anyone applying for British citizenship. From 2 April 2007 this requirement was extended to include people seeking to permanently settle in the UK.

TEST FACTS

● Applicants are given 45 minutes to complete the test

● The test is made up of 24 multiple choice questions

● Questions are chosen at random by computer

● The pass mark is 75% (18 questions correct out of 24)

● Each attempt to pass the test costs £34

● The test is conducted at over 130 Life in the UK Test Centres across the UK

● Applicants sit the test using a computer, which is provided by the test centre

● 68.5% of applicants pass the test (as at 30 June 2007)

The Home Office has indicated that the current price to take the test (£34) is under review. Be aware that this price is likely to increase.

If you are having difficulty reading the English in this book then you should consider attending combined English language (ESOL) and citizenship classes instead of taking the Life in the UK Test. Completing one of these classes will allow you to qualify for settlement or citizenship in the same way as passing the Life in the UK Test.

Most local further education or community colleges run these courses. However, the courses are extremely popular and often have waiting lists. To find out where courses are available in your area contact the Life in the UK Test Helpline on 0800 015 4245.

There are different types of ESOL courses, however only the combined ESOL for citizenship courses can be used instead of taking the Life in the UK Test. Make sure that the course you choose is the correct one.

Who is exempt from taking the test?

Some people do not need to take the test. It is important to note that you don't need to take the test if you are in any of the following circumstances:

● You are under 18 years of age or over 65 years of age

● You have a significant physical or mental health condition. This condition must prevent you from studying for or taking the test, or from studying for an ESOL qualification.

 If you have a visual or hearing impairment then this will not exempt you from the test. Most test centres are well equipped to assist people with such disabilities. Check with your local test centre to see if they can accommodate you. If they can not, then contact the Home Office for guidance on completing your application for settlement or citizenship.

There are also additional exemptions that apply for some people who are taking the test as part of an application for settlement in the UK.

HOW TO PASS YOUR TEST

Step 1: Book your test

Your first step should be to book an appointment to sit the Life in the UK Test. Tests are carried out at over 90 test centres throughout the UK. You can find the test centre closest to you by visiting **www.lifeintheuk.net/book** or by calling the Life in the UK Test Helpline on 0800 015 4245.

You should expect to wait a few weeks for your test appointment. This is normal and provides you with a date to focus your study towards.

In 2006, the average waiting time for a test was 15 days. Make sure you plan ahead and book your test early.

Step 2: Study the materials

Once you have a test appointment, you can start to study with that date in mind as a goal.

All the questions that can be asked in the Life in the UK Test are based on the official study materials provided by the Home Office. These have been fully reproduced in this guide.

Before you start your study, note that your official test will only ask questions based on **Chapters 2, 3, 4, 5 and 6** of the Home Office publication. The questions in this book are also drawn **only from those chapters.**

Step 3: Take practice tests

Once you've finished thoroughly reviewing the study materials you should check if you are ready to take the official test by completing several practice tests from this book.

There are ten practice tests in this book. Each of the practice tests is different and contains 24 unique questions. Each test contains questions covering all parts of the study materials.

When you sit your official test you will be given 45 minutes to complete the test. So when you take a practice test you should allow yourself the same time. The pass mark in the official test is at least 75% – or only six incorrect answers. Again, this is what you should aim to score when you take a practice test.

If you can consistently score at least 75% and finish a test within 45 minutes then you are ready to take your official test.

If you do not pass the practice tests satisfactorily, or do not feel confident enough to sit your official test, then you should continue your study. If you do not have sufficient time left before your official test to do more study, then you may be able to reschedule your test appointment. Most test centres are happy to do this if you give them reasonable notice. However, there may be a £10 administration fee if you give less than seven days notice. Contact your test centre for more details.

Some of the questions asked in your test may be specific to the part of Britain where you are taking your test. If you are taking the test in Scotland, Wales or Northern Ireland then you should make sure you understand the information in the study materials that is specific to where you live.

The answers for each test are provided in the back of the book. To make scoring easier, photocopy or cut out the marking sheet and use this to record your answers. By doing this you can easily match the marking sheet alongside the answer tables.

Once you've finished testing yourself using the questions in this book, you can go online and access further tests with our free subscription offer.

Visit **www.lifeintheuk.net** to redeem this offer.

Additional questions can also be found in our separate publication '*Life in the UK Test: Practice Questions*'.

Do not memorise questions. The practice questions contained in this book are intended to help you test your understanding of the study materials and check if you are ready to take the official test. All the questions are in the same format as the official test questions. However, the Home Office regularly revises the questions used in the Life in the UK Test. Therefore the wording of questions will be different in the official test.

Do not attempt the official test without fully reading the study materials.

Step 4: Take and pass your test

Before you leave for the test centre, make sure you bring photographic ID with you. This ID must be valid and not expired. The following types are acceptable forms of photographic ID.

● a passport (from your country of origin)

● a UK photocard driving licence

● one of the following Home Office travel documents: a Convention Travel Document (CTD), a Certificate of Identity Document (CID) or a Stateless Person Document (SPD)

● an Immigration Status Document, endorsed with a UK Residence Permit and bearing a photo of the holder

 If you do not bring acceptable photographic ID then the test supervisor will not allow you to sit the test.

If you have had previous contact with the Home Office (for example, when applying for an extension of stay) then you will have been issued with a Home Office reference number. You should take this number with you when you take your test, and provide it to the test supervisor when asked.

When you arrive at the test centre you will need to register your details and pay your test fee.

You will take the test using a computer provided at the test centre. You will be allowed to run through a few practice questions so that you are familiar with the test software. Some applicants worry that they do not know the answers for the practice questions, however the results of the practice questions do not affect your end result. The whole process leading up to the test itself may take some time due to the official nature of the test.

Make sure you listen carefully when the test supervisor explains how to use the test software. It is important that you know how to use it. If you are unsure then ask the test supervisor for help. As each applicant's test is begun individually by the test supervisor, your test will not begin until you say that you are ready.

The test consists of 24 multiple choice questions. Questions are chosen at random from a selection of about 400 questions.

Once the test begins you will have 45 minutes to complete it. This is plenty of time if you have studied the materials. In 2007, Ufi announced that one in three candidates completed the test within 15 minutes and 80% of candidates completed the test within 30 minutes. You will be able to review and change the answers to your questions at any stage during the test.

If you pass then you will be given a Pass Notification Letter. This is an important document and must be attached to your settlement or citizenship application.

You will not be able to get a replacement Pass Notification Letter if you lose it. Make sure you keep it in a safe place.

If you don't pass then you can take the test again, however you will need to book and pay for another appointment. You must wait at least seven days before retaking your test.

If you are taking the Life in the UK Test because you want to settle in the UK go to page 17. If you are applying for British citizenship go to page 21.

CHECKLIST

There are a lot of things that you need to remember to do for the Life in the UK Test. Avoid problems and get organised by completing this checklist.

☐ Test appointment booked

Book your test by visiting **www.lifeintheuk.net/book** or by calling the Life in the UK Test Helpline on **0800 015 4245**

Test Date   Time

Test Centre Address

Phone

☐ Finished reading study materials

☐ Completed Practice Tests

☐ Completed Free Online Practice Tests

☐ Checked latest tips and advice at **www.lifeintheuk.net**

☐ Valid photographic ID arranged

☐ Test centre location and travel route confirmed

SETTLING IN BRITAIN

If you've decided to settle in Britain then you're in good company. Every year over 100,000 people apply for the right to stay in the UK permanently.

Although it is possible to stay in the UK by applying to renew your existing visa, most people will apply to get a visa for *indefinite leave to remain* (ILR). This type of visa is sometimes called *permanent residency or settlement* – it all refers to the same thing. ILR will allow you to stay in the UK for as long as you want, without ever needing to apply for extension or renewal.

Before you start applying for indefinite leave to remain, check that you satisfy the qualifying requirements. This is important. If you don't meet the requirements, and your application is not successful, you will not get a refund of your application fee.

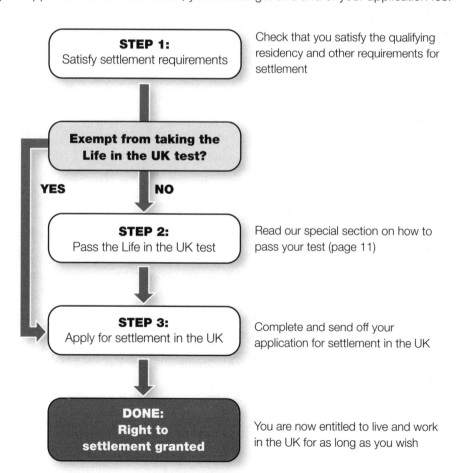

STEP 1:
Satisfy settlement requirements

Check that you satisfy the qualifying residency and other requirements for settlement

Exempt from taking the Life in the UK test?

YES   **NO**

STEP 2:
Pass the Life in the UK test

Read our special section on how to pass your test (page 11)

STEP 3:
Apply for settlement in the UK

Complete and send off your application for settlement in the UK

DONE:
Right to
settlement granted

You are now entitled to live and work in the UK for as long as you wish

Three Steps to Settlement

Step 1: Satisfy settlement requirements

There are several ways to get indefinite leave to remain. Deciding which one is best for you will depend on your circumstances. This can be a complicated decision as there are many exceptions and policy changes regularly. The best place to start is to get the latest information and forms by visiting **www.lifeintheuk.net/applying_for_ilr/**

You must have lived in the UK for a certain amount of time before you can apply for ILR. This is called the qualifying period. This is one of the basic requirements that everyone must satisfy. The table below lists some of the broad application categories and their qualifying periods.

Application Type	Qualifying Period
Marriage or Unmarried partners	2 years
Ex HM Forces	4 years
Highly Skilled Migrant Programme or work permit	5 years
UK Ancestry	5 years
Investors or Business	5 years
Writers, composers and artists	5 years
Long residence (Lawful)	10 years
Long residence (Unlawful)	14 years

Step 2: Pass the Life in the UK Test

If you satisfy the requirements for settlement then you will need to take the Life in the UK Test.

There are special exceptions for the test if you are applying for settlement only. These exemptions apply to:

- Foreign and Commonwealth citizens on discharge from HM Forces (including Ghurkhas where the qualifying period has been met)
- Spouses of foreign and Commonwealth citizens on discharge from HM Forces (including Ghurkhas)
- Bereaved spouses, bereaved unmarried partners and bereaved civil partners
- Parents, grandparents and other dependent relatives living in exceptionally compassionate circumstances, who are joining a person already present and settled in the UK

- Retired persons of independent means

- Spouses, civil partners, unmarried or same sex partners of British citizens or persons settled in the UK, who are permanent members of HM Diplomatic Service; staff members of the British Council on a tour of duty abroad; and staff members of the Department for International Development

- EEA/EU nationals

- Turkish ECAA nationals

Note that these exemptions only apply to people seeking settlement. If you wish to subsequently apply for British citizenship then these exemptions do not apply.

Learn how to pass your test by reading our step-by-step process on page 11.

Step 3: Apply for settlement in the UK

Once you've passed the Life in the UK Test (or confirmed your exemption) you can start the formal process of applying for settlement. You should already know the category that you are using for your application from Step 1. In this case, it's just a simple matter of completing the correct form.

When applying for settlement, you usually have to compile a large amount of supporting documentation and evidence. This is particularly true if you are applying on the grounds of marriage or unmarried partners.

Your supporting documentation is extremely important. Your application form will include a checklist of all the documents that should be included. Make sure you follow this closely.

When you submit your application you may have a choice of postal service or premium service. Premium service applications allow you to present your application in a face-to-face appointment with a case worker. These applications generally result in a decision being made on the same day. Details about how to book an appointment are printed on application forms.

The earliest that you can apply for ILR is 28 days before completing your qualifying period. Do not send your application any earlier than this, otherwise your application will be rejected. You will lose your application fee and will need to pay this again to reapply.

If you intend to use the premium service then make sure you leave at least one week between taking the Life in the UK test and attending your appointment. If your appointment is sooner than one week after your test date then the Home Office may be unable to complete your application on the same day.

Postal applications require you to send your application and documentation into the Home Office by post. During this time you will not have access to your passport and other documentation. For many people, the postal application process is unappealing. The prospect of sending away your personal documentation is a serious inconvenience. If it is important that you always have access to your documents then the premium service may be a better option for you.

BECOMING A BRITISH CITIZEN

There are several ways of becoming a British citizen, however, the most common is called Naturalisation. This is the process used by a person who wants to become a British citizen but was not born in Britain or has no qualifying British ancestral background.

This section provides you with an overview of the naturalisation requirements. It also discusses the issues and considerations you need to be aware of before you make your application.

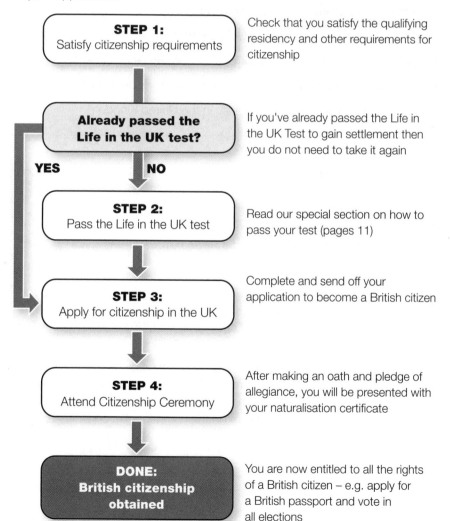

STEP 1:
Satisfy citizenship requirements

Check that you satisfy the qualifying residency and other requirements for citizenship

Already passed the Life in the UK test?

If you've already passed the Life in the UK Test to gain settlement then you do not need to take it again

YES   NO

STEP 2:
Pass the Life in the UK test

Read our special section on how to pass your test (pages 11)

STEP 3:
Apply for citizenship in the UK

Complete and send off your application to become a British citizen

STEP 4:
Attend Citizenship Ceremony

After making an oath and pledge of allegiance, you will be presented with your naturalisation certificate

DONE:
British citizenship obtained

You are now entitled to all the rights of a British citizen – e.g. apply for a British passport and vote in all elections

Four Steps to British Citizenship

Step 1: Satisfy citizenship requirements

Before you start applying for citizenship by naturalisation, you must check that you satisfy the requirements. You must meet ALL of the requirements below. This is important. If you don't meet the requirements, and your application is not successful, you will not get a refund of your application fee.

- Are aged 18 or over when you apply

- Are of good character and sound mind

- Intend to continue living in the United Kingdom

- Have good English (or Welsh or Scottish Gaelic) language skills

- Have lived in the United Kingdom for the qualifying residential period

- Have sufficient knowledge about life in the United Kingdom

Each of these requirements is discussed in more detail in the following sections.

These requirements may change so be sure to check our website **www.lifeintheuk.net/updates** for the latest updates.

Age

You must be at least 18 years old when you apply for citizenship by naturalisation. If you are under this age your application will be declined.

There are different processes for citizenship applications by people under 18. These applications are subject to a number of conditions and are not discussed in this book. You should consult the Home Office or discuss your application with a qualified immigration consultant. A list of qualified immigration consultants is available from **www.oisc.org.uk**

Character

The Home Office will carry out various checks on your background to confirm you are of good character.

Your application must show that you have shown respect for the rights and freedoms of the United Kingdom, observed its laws and fulfilled your duties and obligations as a resident.

For example, simple obligations like your income tax and National Insurance obligations will be checked, as will infringements of the law. These checks will include details of all civil proceedings that have resulted in a court order being made against you.

Your application is unlikely to succeed if you have a recurring history of criminal offences or if you are an undischarged bankrupt. The Home Office uses its discretion when reviewing criminal offences. The amount of time since the offence and any reoccurrence are considered when assessing your application.

Future intentions

The Home Office expects that new British citizens will continue to remain in the United Kingdom. You will be asked to confirm this when you complete your application form. If you do not intend to stay in the United Kingdom after gaining citizenship then you must provide a good explanation. The only acceptable explanation is that you intend to start work for an overseas based organisation that has an association with the United Kingdom. This indicates that you at least intend to continue being an active citizen of the United Kingdom.

Language

British citizens are expected to be able to speak English to a high standard so that they can integrate and participate in British society. If you pass the Life in the UK Test then this shows that you already have good English skills and will not be required to do any further language tests.

Qualifying residence

You must have lived in the United Kingdom for a certain amount of time before you can apply for citizenship. You must have lived in the United Kingdom for at least five years, or for at least three years if you are applying on the basis that you are married to a British citizen.

You MUST have been physically present in the United Kingdom on the day five years before the date of your application (or three years if you are applying on the basis that you are married to a British citizen). The application date is the date on which it is received by the Home Office. For example, if you apply on 1 December 2006 then you must have been in the United Kingdom on 1 December 2001. You should have a dated immigration stamp in your passport from when you first arrived in the UK. This will help you to calculate your application date with confidence.

If you are applying on the basis that you have lived in the United Kingdom for five years you should also have been granted permanent residency (sometimes called Indefinite Leave to Remain) in the United Kingdom more than 12 months prior to the date of your application. In addition, you must not have breached any immigration laws during your residence.

It is very important that you satisfy the qualifying residence requirements. Each year thousands of applications are automatically rejected because they do not meet these requirements. Read this section carefully!

If you have spent a lot of time outside the United Kingdom then this may count against you. The Home Office has clear guidelines on what it considers an acceptable amount of time that you can be absent from the United Kingdom.

You must not have been absent for more than 90 days in the last 12 months. Also you must not have been absent for more than 450 days in the five years prior to the date of your application. If you are applying on the basis that you are married to a British citizen then you must not have been absent for more than 270 days in the last three years prior to the date of your application.

Other Considerations

Before you apply for British citizenship you should be aware of all the implications of becoming a British citizen. Although you will gain all the rights and privileges of being a citizen you will also be expected to fulfil certain duties and obligations as required by law.

Some countries will automatically revoke your citizenship when you become a citizen of another country. You should check with your nearest Consulate or High Commission for your home country. Once you give up your existing citizenship you may not be able to get it back again.

Step 2: Pass the Life in the UK Test

If you satisfy the requirements for British citizenship then you will need to take the Life in the UK Test.

Learn how to pass your test by reading our step-by-step process on page 11.

If you have already had to sit the Life in the UK Test as part of your application to settle in the UK then you do not need to retake the test.

Step 3: Submit your Citizenship Application

Once you've passed the test and gathered all the necessary documentation you can start the process of applying for citizenship.

Be careful that you correctly submit your application. It is not possible to get a refund for incorrect applications. Thousands of citizenship applications are rejected each year for reasons that could have easily been avoided.

The most common reason for unsuccessful citizenship applications is that the residency requirements are not satisfied. In particular, make sure you satisfy the requirement that you were in the UK five years (or three years if you are married to a British citizen) before the date of your application. Be careful that you work out your application date correctly.

Top Five Reasons for Unsuccessful Applications

Residency requirements not satisfied: 40%

- Application sent too early
- Absent from the UK for too long

Age or language requirements not satisfied: 28%

- Applicant is under or over age limit
- Insufficient knowledge of English

Delay in replying to Home Office enquiries: 14%

- Additional information not supplied when requested
- Unable to contact applicant

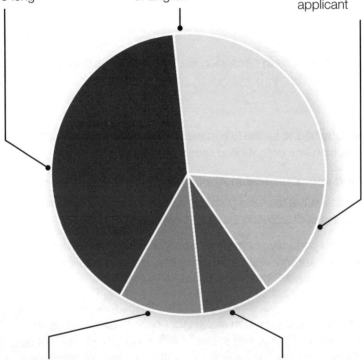

Not of good character: 10%

- Considered a threat to national security
- Recurring criminal history

Application not correctly completed: 8%

- Application fee not paid
- Unacceptable documentation submitted
- Late or improper application

Source: Home Office 2006

A good way to check that your submission is complete is to use the Nationality Checking Service (NCS). The service has two benefits:

1. Your application is checked to make sure it has been completed correctly and that all required supporting documentation is attached.

2. Valuable documents (such as passports) are photocopied and returned.

This service is offered by many local councils and is very popular. It should cost about £40 to submit your application using the service.

Check **www.lifeintheuk.net/ncs** to find your closest participating council.

If you are planning to travel abroad you should use the Nationality Checking Service to submit your Citizenship Application. They will check and photocopy your passport and return it to you before sending off your application.

Step 4: Attend your Citizenship Ceremony

If your application for citizenship is accepted then you will receive a Citizenship Invitation by post. You will be asked to attend your citizenship ceremony. This is the last step in the process and afterwards you'll officially be a British citizen.

Your Citizenship Invitation letter will contain all the information you need to book your ceremony.

Citizenship ceremonies are hosted by the Superintendent Registrar and usually local dignitaries will also attend. The ceremonies are normally attended by a number of other new citizens. You will be allowed to bring a limited number of guests to the ceremony.

The format of the ceremony will vary depending on the venue. In most cases there will be a welcome speech. Then you will be asked to stand and swear the oath of allegiance or, if you prefer, to speak the affirmation of allegiance. You will also be asked to take the Citizenship Pledge. Some ceremonies will perform the oaths, affirmations and pledges as a group, others will go around each member of the group individually.

Oath of allegiance

I (name) swear by Almighty God ...

... that on becoming a British citizen, I will be faithful and bear true allegiance to Her Majesty Queen Elizabeth the Second, her Heirs and Successors, according to law.

Affirmation of allegiance

I (name) do solemnly and sincerely affirm ...

... that on becoming a British citizen, I will be faithful and bear true allegiance to Her Majesty Queen Elizabeth the Second, her Heirs and Successors, according to law.

Citizenship Pledge

I will give my loyalty to the United Kingdom and respect its rights and freedoms. I will uphold its democratic values. I will observe its laws faithfully and fulfil my duties and obligations as a British citizen.

The national anthem will then be played and may be sung as a group – depending on the organisation of the ceremony. Either way, all British citizens should know the words. It is very short – only 29 words long.

God Save the Queen

God save our gracious Queen,

Long live our noble Queen,

God save the Queen:

Send her victorious,

Happy and glorious,

Long to reign over us:

God save the Queen.

Finally, you will be presented with your citizenship certificate and an information pack. Many people like to remember this formal occasion and take photographs – this is definitely encouraged! It has taken a long time to get to this point so make sure you enjoy it.

 Professional photographers may attend your ceremony and offer good quality photographs. Alternatively if you bring your own camera there will be many people at the event who will be happy to take your photograph.

Applying for a British passport

Now that you are officially a British citizen, you can apply for a British passport. This is a relatively simple matter. However, the increase in passport fraud and identity theft has meant that there are more checks to process new applications.

The Identity and Passport Service (IPS) have introduced interviews for all first-time applicants for a British passport. The interview is to verify your identity by getting you to confirm details about your background and past history. Details about booking an interview will be sent to you after your application has been received by the IPS. The interview should take 30 minutes and is free of charge. IPS recommend that you allow six weeks to obtain a passport, and not to book any travel arrangements until the new passport is received.

You can get an application form for a British passport using the following methods:

● Collect a form from selected Post Office® branches and Worldchoice travel agents

● Fill in the online application form request to receive a form in the post

● Call the 24-hour Passport Adviceline 0870 521 0410

● Go online and submit your details using the online application form at **www.passport.gov.uk/passport_online.asp**

If you fill in your form online you get the benefit of interactive help while completing your form. It's also much easier to correct mistakes. Once you've finished submitting your details online, the form is printed and sent to you. All you need to do then is attach your supporting documents and submit your application.

Before sending your application, make sure your photographs comply with new biometric regulations. There are strict guidelines for photographs and it is recommended that you visit an experienced passport photo retailer to have your photograph taken.

There are several different ways that you can submit your passport application. These have different turnaround times and fees. Full details of these fees will be included with your application form.

Look out for the 'Check and Send' service that is available at selected Post Office® branches and Worldchoice travel agents throughout the UK. This is very popular – almost half of all people making a UK Passport application use this service. Your application is checked for errors and given priority treatment by the Identity and Passport Service. The service costs £7 and includes the postage costs for your application.

STUDY MATERIALS

The following section contains all the official study materials that you need to revise for the test, as published by the Home Office. If you would like to learn more about any of the topics discussed in this section then visit **www.lifeintheuk.net**

CHAPTER 2:
A CHANGING SOCIETY

In this chapter you will learn about how British society has changed in recent times. The chapter mainly focuses on how different groups have contributed to society since the end of the Second World War. Think about why migrants wanted to come to Britain, but also consider why Britain wanted and needed new immigrants. Concentrate on how women have gained more rights and responsibilities, particularly in politics, education and the workplace. Also think about differences that have developed in how women contribute in their more traditional family roles, especially in terms of childcare. When reading the section on children and young people consider how families have changed in Britain. Also focus on the challenges that face children and young people today as they progress through the education system and become young adults.

Some of the information in this chapter is now out of date due to changes in law and regulations. However, only published facts, as included in this chapter, will be used for your test. Read more about this on page 207.

In this chapter there is information about:

● Migration to Britain
- The long history of immigration to the United Kingdom
- Different reasons why people migrated to the UK
- Basic changes in immigration patterns over the last 30 years

● The changing role of women
- Changes to family structures and women's rights since the 19th century
- Women's campaigns for rights, including the right to vote, in the late 19th and early 20th centuries

- Discrimination against women in the workplace and in education
- Changing attitudes to women working, and responsibilities of men and women in the home

● Children, family and young people
- The identity, interests, tastes and lifestyle patterns of children and young people
- Education and work
- Health hazards: cigarettes, alcohol and illegal drugs
- Young people's political and social attitudes

Migration to Britain

Many people living in Britain today have their origins in other countries. They can trace their roots to regions throughout the world such as Europe, the Middle East, Africa, Asia and the Caribbean. In the distant past, invaders came to Britain, seized land and stayed. More recently, people come to Britain to find safety, jobs and a better life.

Britain is proud of its tradition of offering safety to people who are escaping persecution and hardship. For example, in the 16th and 18th centuries, Huguenots (French Protestants) came to Britain to escape religious persecution in France. In the mid-1840s there was a terrible famine in Ireland and many Irish people migrated to Britain. Many Irish men became labourers and helped to build canals and railways across Britain.

From 1880 to 1910, a large number of Jewish people came to Britain to escape racist attacks (called 'pogroms') in what was then called the Russian Empire and from the countries now called Poland, Ukraine and Belarus.

Migration since 1945

After the Second World War (1939–45), there was a huge task of rebuilding Britain. There were not enough people to do the work, so the British government encouraged workers from Ireland and other parts of Europe to come to the UK to help with the reconstruction. In 1948, people from the West Indies were also invited to come and work.

During the 1950s, there was still a shortage of labour in the UK. The UK encouraged immigration in the 1950s for economic reasons and many industries advertised for workers from overseas. For example, centres were set up in the West Indies to recruit people to drive buses. Textile and engineering firms from the north of England and the Midlands sent agents to India and Pakistan to find workers. For about 25 years, people from the West Indies, India, Pakistan, and later Bangladesh, travelled to work and settle in Britain.

The number of people migrating from these areas fell in the late 1960s and early 70s because the Government passed new laws to restrict immigration to Britain, although immigrants from 'old' Commonwealth countries such as Australia, New Zealand and Canada did not have to face such strict controls.

During this time, however, the UK was able to help a large number of refugees. In 1972 the UK accepted thousands of people of Indian origin who had been forced to leave Uganda. Another programme to help people from Vietnam was introduced in the late 1970s. Since 1979, more than 25,000 refugees from South

East Asia have been allowed to settle in the UK.

In the 1980s the largest immigrant groups came from the United States, Australia, South Africa and New Zealand. In the early 1990s, groups of people from the former Soviet Union came to Britain looking for a new and safer way of life. Since 1994 there has been a global rise in mass migration for both political and economic reasons.

REVISION QUESTIONS

Check your understanding of this section by completing the questions below.
Check your answers on page 191.

1 List some of the reasons why migrants have come to the UK

ANSWER:

2 What work did migrant Irish labourers do during the Irish famine in the mid 1840s?

ANSWER:

3 In 1948, what were immigrants from Ireland and the West Indies invited into the UK to do?

ANSWER:

4 Name two countries that the UK admitted refugees from during the 1970s

ANSWER:

5 Name the four largest immigrant groups that came to the UK during the 1980s

ANSWER:

6 Why did Protestant Huguenots from France come to Britain?

ANSWER:

7 During the 1950s, bus driver recruitment centres were set up in which area?

ANSWER:

8 During the 1950s, textile and engineering firms from the UK sent recruitment agents to which two countries?

ANSWER:

The changing role of women

In 19th-century Britain, families were usually large and in many poorer homes men, women and children all contributed towards the family income. Although they made an important economic contribution, women in Britain had fewer rights than men. Until 1857, a married woman had no right to divorce her husband. Until 1882, when a woman got married, her earnings, property and money automatically belonged to her husband.

In the late 19th and early 20th centuries, an increasing number of women campaigned and demonstrated for greater rights and, in particular, the right to vote. They became known as 'Suffragettes'. These protests decreased during the First World War because women joined in the war effort and therefore did a much greater variety of work than they had before. When the First World War ended in 1918, women over the age of 30 were finally given the right to vote and to stand for election to Parliament. It was not until 1928 that women won the right to vote at 21, at the same age as men.

Despite these improvements, women still faced discrimination in the workplace. For example, it was quite common for employers to ask women to leave their jobs when they got married. Many jobs were closed to women and it was difficult for women to enter universities. During the 1960s and 1970s there was increasing pressure from women for equal rights. Parliament passed new laws giving women the right to equal pay and prohibiting employers from discriminating against women because of their sex (see also chapter 6).

Women in Britain today

Women in Britain today make up 51% of the population and 45% of the workforce. These days girls leave school, on average, with better qualifications than boys and there are now more women than men at university.

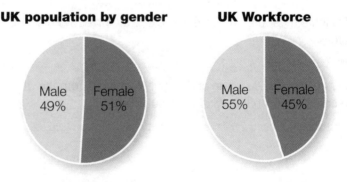

UK population by gender

Male 49% Female 51%

UK Workforce

Male 55% Female 45%

Employment opportunities for women are now much greater than they were in the past. Although women continue to be employed in traditional female areas such as healthcare, teaching, secretarial and retail work, there is strong evidence that attitudes are changing, and women are now active in a much wider range of work than before. Research shows that very few people today believe that women in Britain should stay at home and not go out to work. Today, almost three-quarters of women with school-age children are in paid work.

In most households, women continue to have the main responsibility for childcare and housework. There is evidence that there is now greater equality in homes and that more men are taking some responsibility for raising the family and doing housework. Despite this progress, many people believe that more needs to be done to achieve greater equality for women. There are still examples of discrimination against women, particularly in the workplace, despite the laws that exist to prevent it. Women still do not always have the same access to promotion and better-paid jobs. The average hourly pay rate for women is 20% less than for men, and after leaving university most women still earn less than men.

REVISION QUESTIONS

Check your understanding of this section by completing the questions below. Check your answers on page 191.

9	What year did women in the UK gain the right to divorce their husband?
	ANSWER:

10	What year did women first get the right to vote?
	ANSWER:

11	What percentage of the workforce are women?
	ANSWER:

12	Are there more men or women in study at university?
	ANSWER:

13	In what year did women get the right to vote at the same age as men?
	ANSWER:

14	What proportion of women with children (of school age) also work?
	ANSWER:

Children, family and young people

In the UK, there are almost 15 million children and young people up to the age of 19. This is almost one-quarter of the UK population.

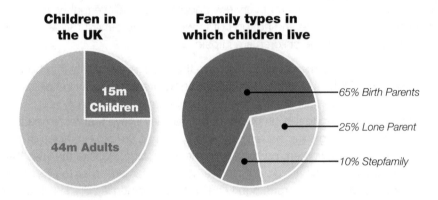

Children in the UK

15m Children

44m Adults

Family types in which children live

65% Birth Parents

25% Lone Parent

10% Stepfamily

Over the last 20 years, family patterns in Britain have been transformed because of the changing attitudes towards divorce and separation. Today, 65% of children live with both birth parents, almost 25% live in lone-parent families, and 10% live within a stepfamily. Most children in Britain receive weekly pocket money from their parents and many get extra money for doing jobs around the house.

Children in the UK do not play outside the home as much as they did in the past. Part of the reason for this is increased home entertainment such as television, videos and computers. There is also increased concern for children's safety and there are many stories in newspapers about child molestation by strangers, but there is no evidence that this kind of danger is increasing.

Young people have different identities, interests and fashions to older people. Many young people move away from their family home when they become adults but this varies from one community to another.

Education

The law states that children between the ages of 5 and 16 must attend school. The tests that pupils take are very important, and in England and Scotland children take national tests in English, mathematics and science when they are 7, 11 and 14 years old. (In Wales, teachers assess children's progress when they are 7 and 11 and they take a national test at the age of 14.) The tests give important information about children's progress and achievement, the subjects they are doing well in and the areas where they need extra help.

Most young people take the General Certificate of Secondary Education (GCSE), or, in Scotland, Scottish Qualifications Authority (SQA) Standard Grade examinations when they are 16. At 17 and 18, many take vocational qualifications, General Certificates of Education at an Advanced level (AGCEs), AS level units or Higher/Advanced Higher Grades in Scotland. Schools and colleges will expect good GCSE or SQA Standard Grade results before allowing a student to enrol on an AGCE or Scottish Higher/Advanced Higher course.

AS levels are Advanced Subsidiary qualifications gained by completing three AS units. Three AS units are considered as one-half of an AGCE. In the second part of the course, three more AS units can be studied to complete the AGCE qualification.

Many people refer to AGCEs by the old name of A levels. AGCEs are the traditional route for entry to higher education courses, but many higher education students enter with different kinds of qualifications.

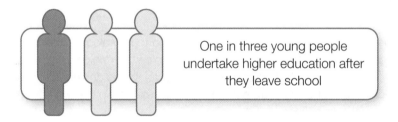

One in three young people undertake higher education after they leave school

One in three young people now go on to higher education at college or university. Some young people defer their university entrance for a year and take a 'gap year'. This year out of education often includes voluntary work and travel overseas. Some young people work to earn and save money to pay for their university fees and living expenses.

People over 16 years of age may also choose to study at Colleges of Further Education or Adult Education Centres. There is a wide range of academic and vocational courses available as well as courses which develop leisure interests and skills. Contact your local college for details.

Work

It is common for young people to have a part-time job while they are still at school. It is thought there are 2 million children at work at any one time. The most common jobs are newspaper delivery and work in supermarkets and newsagents. Many parents believe that part-time work helps children to become more independent as well as providing them (and sometimes their families) with extra income.

There are laws about the age when children can take up paid work (usually not before 14), the type of work they can do and the number of hours they can work (see **www.worksmart.org.uk** for more information).

It is very important to note that there are concerns for the safety of children who work illegally or who are not properly supervised and the employment of children is strictly controlled by law (see chapter 6).

Health hazards

Many parents worry that their children may misuse drugs and addictive substances.

Smoking

Although cigarette smoking has fallen in the adult population, more young people are smoking, and more school age girls smoke than boys. From 1 October 2007, it is illegal to sell tobacco products to anyone under 18 years old. Smoking is generally not allowed in public buildings and work places throughout the UK.

Alcohol

Young people under the age of 18 are not allowed to buy alcohol in Britain, but there is concern about the age some young people start drinking alcohol and the amount of alcohol they drink at one time, known as 'binge drinking'. It is illegal to be drunk in public and there are now more penalties to help control this problem, including on-the-spot fines.

Illegal drugs

As in most countries, it is illegal to possess drugs such as heroin, cocaine, ecstasy, amphetamines and cannabis. Current statistics show that half of all young adults, and about a third of the population as a whole, have used illegal drugs at one time or another.

There is a strong link between the use of hard drugs (e.g. crack cocaine and heroin) and crime, and also hard drugs and mental illness. The misuse of drugs has a huge social and financial cost for the country. This is a serious issue and British society needs to find an effective way of dealing with the problem.

Young people's political and social attitudes

Young people in Britain can vote in elections from the age of 18. In the 2001 general election, however, only 1 in 5 first-time voters used their vote. There has been a great debate over the reasons for this. Some researchers think that one reason is that young people are not interested in the political process.

Although most young people show little interest in party politics, there is strong evidence that many are interested in specific political issues such as the environment and cruelty to animals.

In 2003 a survey of young people in England and Wales showed that they believe the five most important issues in Britain were crime, drugs, war/terrorism, racism and health. The same survey asked young people about their participation in political and community events. They found that 86% of young people had taken part in some form of community event over the past year, and 50% had taken part in fund-raising or collecting money for charity. Similar results have been found in surveys in Scotland and Northern Ireland. Many children first get involved in these activities while at school where they study citizenship as part of the National Curriculum.

REVISION QUESTIONS

Check your understanding of this section by completing the questions below.
Check your answers on page 191.

15 How many young people (up to the age of 19) are there in the UK?
ANSWER:

16 What percentage of children do not live with both birth parents (i.e. live in single parent families or stepfamilies)?
ANSWER:

17 How often do most children in the UK receive their pocket money?
ANSWER:

18 What percentage of children in the UK live with both birth parents?
ANSWER:

19 How many children (under 18) are estimated to be working in the UK at any time?
ANSWER:

20 What proportion of young people enrol to go on to higher education?
ANSWER:

21 What is the minimum age for buying tobacco?

ANSWER:

22 In the 2001 general election, what proportion of first time voters actually cast their vote?

ANSWER:

CHAPTER 3:
UK TODAY: A PROFILE

In this chapter you will learn about British society as it is today. The chapter focuses on the people who live in the country now and the things that make them who they are, such as ethnicity, religions, traditions and customs. You should concentrate on where different groups live, particularly various ethnic groups. Britain is a country with a long history and you should note that religions, traditions and customs have developed in many ways in many places. In particular, pay attention to the differences between the four nations of the UK: Wales, Scotland, Northern Ireland and England.

In this chapter there is information about:

● The population of the UK
● The census
● Ethnic diversity
● The regions of Britain
● Religion and religious freedom
● Customs and traditions

POPULATION

In 2005 the population of the United Kingdom was just under 60 million people.

United Kingdom Population 2005

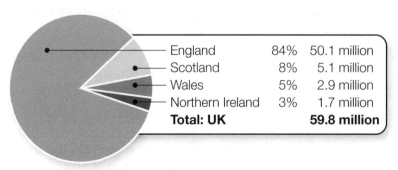

England	84%	50.1 million
Scotland	8%	5.1 million
Wales	5%	2.9 million
Northern Ireland	3%	1.7 million
Total: UK		**59.8 million**

Source: National Statistics

The population has grown by 7.7% since 1971, and growth has been faster in more recent years. Although the general population in the UK has increased in the last 20 years, in some areas such as the North-East and North-West of England there has been a decline. Both the birth rate and the death rate are falling and as a result the UK now has an ageing population. For instance, there are more people over 60 than children under 16. There is also a record number of people aged 85 and over.

The census

A census is a count of the whole population. It also collects statistics on topics such as age, place of birth, occupation, ethnicity, housing, health and marital status.

A census has been taken every ten years since 1801, except during the Second World War. The next census will take place in 2011.

During a census, a form is delivered to every household in the country. This form asks for detailed information about each member of the household and must be completed by law. The information remains confidential and anonymous; it can only be released to the public after 100 years, when many people researching their family history find it very useful. General census information is used to identify population trends and to help planning. More information about the census, the census form and statistics from previous censuses can be found at **www.statistics.gov.uk/census**

Ethnic diversity

The UK population is ethnically diverse and is changing rapidly, especially in large cities such as London, so it is not always easy to get an exact picture of the ethnic origin of all the population from census statistics. Each of the four countries of the UK (England, Wales, Scotland and Northern Ireland) has different customs, attitudes and histories.

People of Indian, Pakistani, Chinese, Black Caribbean, Black African, Bangladeshi and mixed ethnic descent make up 8.3% of the UK population. Today about half the members of these communities were born in the United Kingdom.

There are also considerable numbers of people resident in the UK who are of Irish, Italian, Greek and Turkish Cypriot, Polish, Australian, Canadian, New Zealand and American descent. Large numbers have also arrived since 2004 from the new East European member states of the European Union. These groups are not identified separately in the census statistics in the following diagram.

United Kingdom Population Ethnic Groups 2001

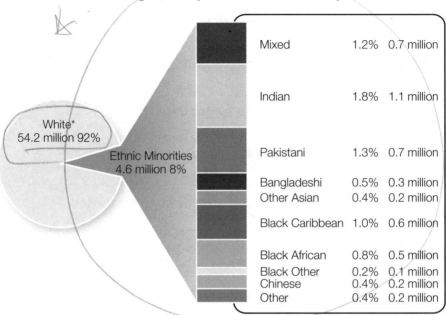

Mixed	1.2%	0.7 million
Indian	1.8%	1.1 million
Pakistani	1.3%	0.7 million
Bangladeshi	0.5%	0.3 million
Other Asian	0.4%	0.2 million
Black Caribbean	1.0%	0.6 million
Black African	0.8%	0.5 million
Black Other	0.2%	0.1 million
Chinese	0.4%	0.2 million
Other	0.4%	0.2 million

White*
54.2 million 92%

Ethnic Minorities
4.6 million 8%

* Includes people of European, Australian, and American descent

Source: National Statistics from the 2001 census

Where do the largest ethnic minority groups live?

The figures from the 2001 census show that most members of the large ethnic minority groups in the UK live in England, where they make up 9% of the total population. 45% of all ethnic minority people live in the London area, where they form nearly one-third of the population (29%). Other areas of England with large ethnic minority populations are the West Midlands, the South East, the North West, and Yorkshire and Humberside.

Proportion of ethnic minority groups in the countries of the UK

England	9%
Wales	2%
Scotland	2%
Northern Ireland	less than 1%

REVISION QUESTIONS

Check your understanding of this section by completing the questions below.
Check your answers on page 191.

23	What was the population of the United Kingdom in 2005?
	ANSWER:

24	How often is a census carried out in the United Kingdom?
	ANSWER:

25	When was the first census carried out in the United Kingdom?
	ANSWER:

26	What are some of the statistics that are collected in a census?
	ANSWER:

27	When will the next UK census be carried out?
	ANSWER:

28	What are the respective populations of England, Scotland, Wales and Northern Ireland?
	ANSWER:

29	How many years must have passed before an individual's census form can be viewed by the public?
	ANSWER:

30	What is the largest ethnic minority in Britain?
	ANSWER:

31	What overall proportion of today's African Caribbean, Pakistani, Indian and Bangladeshi communities in Britain were born in the UK?
	ANSWER:

32	What percentage of the United Kingdom's population is made up of ethnic minorities?
	ANSWER:

33	What percentage of the UK's ethnic minorities live in the London area?
	ANSWER:

34	What percentage of London's residents are ethnic minorities?
	ANSWER:

The nations and regions of the UK

The UK is a medium-sized country. The longest distance on the mainland, from John O'Groats on the north coast of Scotland to Land's End in the south-west corner of England, is about 870 miles (approximately 1,400 kilometres). Most of the population live in towns and cities.

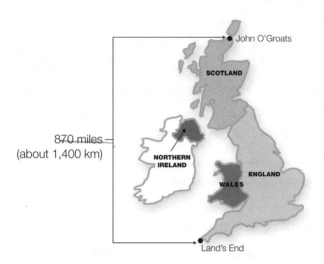

There are many variations in culture and language in the different parts of the United Kingdom. This is seen in differences in architecture, in some local customs, in types of food, and especially in language. The English language has many accents and dialects. These are a clear indication of regional differences in the UK. Well-known dialects in England are Geordie (Tyneside), Scouse (Liverpool) and Cockney (London). Many other languages in addition to English are spoken in the UK, especially in multicultural cities.

In Wales, Scotland and Northern Ireland, people speak different varieties and dialects of English. In Wales, too, an increasing number of people speak Welsh, which is taught in schools and universities. In Scotland Gaelic is spoken in some parts of the Highlands and Islands and in Northern Ireland a few people speak Irish Gaelic. Some of the dialects of English spoken in Scotland show the influence of the old Scottish language, Scots. One of the dialects spoken in Northern Ireland is called Ulster Scots.

REVISION QUESTIONS

Check your understanding of this section by completing the questions below.
Check your answers on page 192.

35 What is the distance from John O'Groats on the north coast of Scotland to Land's End in the south-west corner of England?

ANSWER

36 Where is the Gaelic language spoken?

ANSWER

37 Where is the Welsh language spoken?

ANSWER

38 Where is the Geordie dialect spoken?

ANSWER

39 Where is the Cockney dialect spoken?

ANSWER

40 Where is the Scouse dialect spoken?

ANSWER

Religion

Although the UK is historically a Christian society, everyone has the legal right to practise the religion of their choice. In the 2001 census, just over 75% said they had a religion: 7 out of 10 of these were Christians. There were also a considerable number of people who followed other religions. Although many people in the UK said they held religious beliefs, currently only around 10% of the population attend religious services. More people attend services in Scotland and Northern Ireland than in England and Wales. In London the number of people who attend religious services is increasing.

Religions in the UK

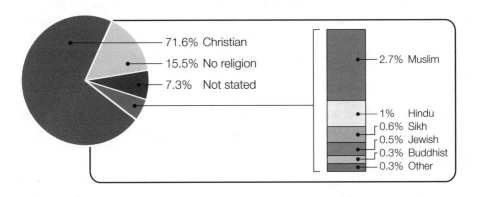

71.6% Christian
15.5% No religion
7.3% Not stated

2.7% Muslim

1%   Hindu
0.6% Sikh
0.5% Jewish
0.3% Buddhist
0.3% Other

Source: National Statistics from the 2001 census

1.	Christian*	71.6%
2.	Muslim	2.7%
3.	Hindu	1.0%
4.	Sikh	0.6%
5.	Jewish	0.5%
6.	Buddhist	0.3%
	Other	0.3%
	Total All	**77.0%**
	No religion	15.5%
	Not stated	7.3%

* 10% of whom are Roman Catholic

The Christian Churches

In England there is a constitutional link between church and state. The official church of the state is the Church of England. The Church of England is called the Anglican Church in other countries and the Episcopal Church in Scotland and in the USA. The Church of England is a Protestant church and has existed since the Reformation in the 1530s. The king or queen (the monarch) is the head, or Supreme Governor, of the Church of England. The monarch is not allowed to marry anyone who is not Protestant. The spiritual leader of the Church of England is the Archbishop of Canterbury. The monarch has the right to select the Archbishop and other senior church officials, but usually the choice is made by the Prime Minister and a committee appointed by the Church. Several Church of England bishops sit in the House of Lords (see chapter 4). The Church of Scotland is Presbyterian, national and free from state control. It has no bishops and is governed for spiritual purposes by a series of courts, so its most senior representative is the Moderator (chairperson) of its annual General Assembly. There is no established church in Wales or in Northern Ireland.

Other Protestant Christian groups in the UK are Baptists, Presbyterians, Methodists and Quakers. 10% of Christians are Roman Catholic (40% in Northern Ireland).

Patron saints

England, Scotland, Wales and Northern Ireland each have a national saint called a patron saint. Each saint has a feast day. In the past these were celebrated as holy days when many people had a day off work. Today these are not public holidays except for 17 March in Northern Ireland.

Patron saints' days

St. David's day, Wales	1 March
St. Patrick's day, Northern Ireland	17 March
St. George's day, England	23 April
St. Andrew's day, Scotland	30 November

There are four 'Bank Holidays' and four other public holidays a year (most people call all these holidays Bank Holidays).

REVISION QUESTIONS

Check your understanding of this section by completing the questions below. Check your answers on page 192.

41	According to the 2001 Census, what percentage of the UK population reported that they had a religion? ANSWER
42	According to the 2001 Census, what proportion of people stated their religion as Christian? ANSWER

43	According to the 2001 Census, what percentage of people stated their religion as Muslim?
	ANSWER
44	Which other name is used to refer to the Church of England?
	ANSWER
45	What is the title of the King or Queen within the Church of England?
	ANSWER
46	Who is the monarch not allowed to marry?
	ANSWER
47	Who appoints the Archbishop of Canterbury?
	ANSWER
48	What percentage of Christians are Roman Catholic?
	ANSWER
49	What and when are the patron saints' days of the four countries of the United Kingdom?
	ANSWER
50	Which of the UK patron saints' days is celebrated with a holiday? Name the country where this is celebrated
	ANSWER

CUSTOMS AND TRADITIONS

Festivals

Throughout the year there are festivals of art, music and culture, such as the Notting Hill Carnival in west London and the Edinburgh Festival. Customs and traditions from various religions, such as Eid ul-Fitr (Muslim), Diwali (Hindu) and Hanukkah (Jewish) are widely recognised in the UK. Children learn about these at school. The main Christian festivals are Christmas and Easter. There are also celebrations of non-religious traditions such as New Year.

The main Christian festivals

Christmas Day

25 December, celebrates the birth of Jesus Christ. It is a public holiday. Many Christians go to church on Christmas Eve (24 December) or on Christmas Day itself. Christmas is also usually celebrated by people who are not Christian. People usually spend the day at home and eat a special meal, which often includes turkey. They give each other gifts, send each other cards and decorate their houses. Many people decorate a tree. Christmas is a special time for children. Very young children believe that an old man, Father Christmas (or Santa Claus), brings them presents during the night. He is always shown in pictures with a long white beard, dressed in red. Boxing Day, 26 December, is the day after Christmas. It is a public holiday.

Other festivals and traditions

New Year

1 January, is a public holiday. People usually celebrate on the night of 31 December. In Scotland, 31 December is called Hogmanay and 2 January is also a public holiday. In Scotland Hogmanay is a bigger holiday for some people than Christmas.

Valentine's Day

14 February, is when lovers exchange cards and gifts. Sometimes people send anonymous cards to someone they secretly admire.

April Fool's Day

1 April, is a day when people play jokes on each other until midday. Often TV and newspapers carry stories intended to deceive credulous viewers and readers.

Mother's Day

The Sunday three weeks before Easter is a day when children send cards or buy gifts for their mothers. Easter is also an important Christian festival.

Halloween

31 October, is a very ancient festival. Young people will often dress up in frightening costumes to play 'trick or treat'. Giving them sweets or chocolates might stop them playing a trick on you. Sometimes people carry lanterns made out of pumpkins with a candle inside.

Guy Fawkes Night

5 November is an occasion when people in Great Britain set off fireworks at home or in special displays. The origin of this celebration was an event in 1605, when a group of Catholics led by Guy Fawkes failed in their plan to kill the Protestant king with a bomb in the Houses of Parliament.

Remembrance Day

11 November, commemorates those who died fighting in World War 1, World War 2 and other wars. Many people wear poppies (a red flower) in memory of those who died. At 11am, there is a two-minute silence.

Sport

Sport of all kinds plays an important part in many people's lives. Football, tennis, rugby and cricket are very popular sports in the UK. There are no United Kingdom teams for football and rugby. England, Scotland, Wales and Northern Ireland have their own teams. Important sporting events include, the Grand National horse race, the Football Association (FA) cup final (and equivalents in Northern Ireland, Scotland and Wales), the Open golf championship and the Wimbledon tennis tournament.

REVISION QUESTIONS

Check your understanding of this section by completing the questions below.
Check your answers on page 192.

51 Name four sports that are popular in the UK.
ANSWER

52 When is Christmas and what does it celebrate?
ANSWER

53 What is traditionally eaten on Christmas Day?
ANSWER

54 When is New Year celebrated in the United Kingdom?
ANSWER

55 When is Valentine's Day, and what traditionally happens that day?
ANSWER

56 When is Mothering Sunday, and what traditionally happens that day?
ANSWER

57 When is April Fool's Day, and what traditionally happens that day?
ANSWER

58 When is Guy Fawkes Night and what does it commemorate?
ANSWER

59 When is Remembrance Day and what does it commemorate?
ANSWER

60 When is Hogmanay celebrated in Scotland?
ANSWER

61 What tradition is observed in the period before Remembrance Day?
ANSWER

CHAPTER 4:
HOW THE UNITED KINGDOM
IS GOVERNED

In this chapter you will learn the basic elements of how government in Britain works. The UK is unusual as it does not have a written constitution. Britain uses institutions, as well as conventions and traditions to provide the guidance usually delivered by a written constitution. The chapter focuses on these institutions and how they work together to provide fair and good government. You need to focus on each institution and how it operates. You will also learn about the ways the government has passed some of its powers down to other institutions, known as devolved administration. A critical development was the establishment of representative assemblies in Wales, Scotland and Northern Ireland.

In addition, you will learn about the political rights enjoyed by every citizen of the UK, such as voting. Finally, the chapter looks at Britain's role in the world and in Europe. It discusses the Commonwealth, the European Union and the United Nations. You should focus on the UK's gradual move into closer cooperation with its European neighbours. Make sure you understand the crucial role that the European Union has in British government, law, politics and the economy.

In this chapter there is information about:

- The system of government
- The monarchy
- The electoral system
- Political parties
- Being a citizen
- Voting

- Contacting your MP
- The UK in Europe and the world
- The European Union
- The Commonwealth
- The United Nations

THE BRITISH CONSTITUTION

As a constitutional democracy, the United Kingdom is governed by a wide range of institutions, many of which provide checks on each other's powers. Most of these institutions are of long standing: they include the monarchy, Parliament, (consisting of the House of Commons and the House of Lords), the office of Prime Minister, the Cabinet, the judiciary, the police, the civil service, and the institutions of local government. More recently, devolved administrations have been set up for Scotland, Wales and Northern Ireland. Together, these formal institutions, laws and conventions form the British Constitution. Some people would argue that the roles of other less formal institutions, such as the media and pressure groups, should also be seen as part of the Constitution.

The British Constitution is not written down in any single document, as are the constitutions of many other countries. This is mainly because the United Kingdom has never had a lasting revolution, like America or France, so our most important institutions have been in existence for hundreds of years. Some people believe that there should be a single document, but others believe that an unwritten constitution allows more scope for institutions to adapt to meet changing circumstances and public expectations.

The monarchy

Queen Elizabeth II is the Head of State of the United Kingdom. She is also the monarch or Head of State for many countries in the Commonwealth. The UK, like Denmark, the Netherlands, Norway, Spain and Sweden, has a constitutional monarchy. This means that the king or queen does not rule the country, but appoints the government which the people have chosen in democratic elections. Although the queen or king can advise, warn and encourage the Prime Minister, the decisions on government policies are made by the Prime Minister and Cabinet.

The Queen has reigned since her father's death in 1952. Prince Charles, the Prince of Wales, her oldest son, is the heir to the throne.

The Queen has important ceremonial roles such as the opening of the new parliamentary session each year. On this occasion the Queen makes a speech that summarises the government's policies for the year ahead.

Government

The system of government in the United Kingdom is a parliamentary democracy.

The UK is divided into 646 parliamentary constituencies and at least every five years voters in each constituency elect their Member of Parliament (MP) in a general election. All of the elected MPs form the House of Commons. Most MPs belong to a political party and the party with the largest number of MPs forms the government.

The law that requires new elections to Parliament to be held at least every five years is so fundamental that no government has sought to change it. A Bill to change it is the only one to which the House of Lords must give its consent.

Some people argue that the power of Parliament is lessened because of the obligation on the United Kingdom to accept the rules of the European Union and the judgments of the European Court, but it was Parliament itself which created these obligations.

The House of Commons

The House of Commons is the more important of the two chambers in Parliament, and its members are democratically elected. Nowadays the Prime Minister and almost all the members of the Cabinet are members of the House of Commons. The members of the House of Commons are called 'Members of Parliament' or MPs for short. Each MP represents a parliamentary constituency, or area of the country: there are 646 of these. MPs have a number of different responsibilities. They represent everyone in their constituency, they help to create new laws, they scrutinise and comment on what the government is doing, and they debate important national issues.

Elections

There must be a general election to elect MPs at least every five years, though they may be held sooner if the Prime Minister so decides. If an MP dies or resigns, there will be another election, called a by-election, in his or her constituency. MPs are elected through a system called 'first past the post'. In each constituency, the candidate who gets the most votes is elected. The government is then formed by the party which wins the majority of constituencies.

The Whips

The Whips are a small group of MPs appointed by their party leaders. They are responsible for discipline in their party and making sure MPs attend the House of Commons to vote. The Chief Whip often attends Cabinet or Shadow Cabinet meetings and arranges the schedule of proceedings in the House of Commons with the Speaker.

European parliamentary elections

Elections for the European Parliament are also held every five years. There are 78 seats for representatives from the UK in the European Parliament and elected members are called Members of the European Parliament (MEPs). Elections to the European Parliament use a system of proportional representation, whereby seats are allocated to each party in proportion to the total votes it won.

The House of Lords

Members of the House of Lords, known as peers, are not elected and do not represent a constituency. The role and membership of the House of Lords have recently undergone big changes. Until 1958 all peers were either 'hereditary', meaning that their titles were inherited, senior judges, or bishops of the Church of England. Since 1958 the Prime Minister has had the power to appoint peers just for their own lifetime. These peers, known as Life Peers, have usually had a distinguished career in politics, business, law or some other profession. This means that debates in the House of Lords often draw on more specialist knowledge than is available to members of the House of Commons. Life Peers are appointed by the Queen on the advice of the Prime Minister, but they include people nominated by the leaders of the other main parties and by an independent Appointments Commission for non-party peers.

QUEEN
Head of State

British Parliament

House of Lords	House of Commons	
	Governing Party	**Opposition & other non-governing parties**
Hereditary Peers	Prime Minister	Leader of the Opposition
Life Peers	Ministers & members of the Cabinet	Shadow Ministers
Senior Bishops & Judges	Whips	Whips
	Other MPs associated with the governing party	Other MPs not associated with the governing party

In the last few years the hereditary peers have lost the automatic right to attend the House of Lords, although they are allowed to elect a few of their number to represent them.

While the House of Lords is usually the less important of the two chambers of Parliament, it is more independent of the government. It can suggest amendments or propose new laws, which are then discussed by the House of Commons. The House of Lords can become very important if the majority of its members will not agree to pass a law for which the House of Commons has voted. The House of Commons has powers to overrule the House of Lords, but these are very rarely used.

The Prime Minister

The Prime Minister (PM) is the leader of the political party in power. He or she appoints the members of the Cabinet and has control over many important public appointments. The official home of the Prime Minister is 10 Downing Street, in central London, near the Houses of Parliament; he or she also has a country house not far from London called Chequers. The Prime Minister can be changed if the MPs in the governing party decide to do so, or if he or she wishes to resign. More usually, the Prime Minister resigns when his or her party is defeated in a general election.

The Cabinet

The Prime Minister appoints about 20 senior MPs to become ministers in charge of departments. These include the Chancellor of the Exchequer, responsible for the economy, the Home Secretary, responsible for law, order and immigration, the Foreign Secretary, and ministers (called 'Secretaries of State') for education, health and defence. The Lord Chancellor, who is the minister responsible for legal affairs, is also a member of the Cabinet but sat in the House of Lords rather than the House of Commons. Following legislation passed in 2005, it is now possible for the Lord Chancellor to sit in the Commons. These ministers form the Cabinet, a small committee which usually meets weekly and makes important decisions about government policy which often then have to be debated or approved by Parliament.

The Opposition

The second largest party in the House of Commons is called the Opposition. The Leader of the Opposition is the person who hopes to become Prime Minister if his or her party wins the next general election. The Leader of the Opposition leads his or her party in pointing out the government's failures and weaknesses; one important opportunity to do this is at Prime Minister's Questions which takes place every week while Parliament is sitting. The Leader of the Opposition also appoints senior Opposition MPs to lead the criticism of government ministers, and together they form the Shadow Cabinet.

The Speaker

Debates in the House of Commons are chaired by the Speaker, the chief officer of the House of Commons. The Speaker is politically neutral. He or she is an MP, elected by fellow MPs to keep order during political debates and to make sure the rules are followed. This includes making sure the Opposition has a guaranteed amount of time to debate issues it chooses. The Speaker also represents Parliament at ceremonial occasions.

REVISION QUESTIONS

Check your understanding of this section by completing the questions below.
Check your answers on page 193.

62 How is the Prime Minister chosen?

ANSWER

63 How often are general elections held in the UK?

ANSWER

64 Where is the Prime Minister's official residence?

ANSWER

65 What is the Cabinet?

ANSWER

66 What is the name of the ministerial position that is responsible for the economy?

ANSWER *chancellor of the Exchequer*

67 What is the name of the ministerial position that is responsible for law, order and immigration?

ANSWER *Home Secretary*

68 What happens to policy & law decisions once they have been agreed by Cabinet?

ANSWER

69 What is the abbreviation MP short for?

ANSWER *Members of palament*

70 Approximately how many MPs are there in Cabinet?

ANSWER *20*

71 How is it decided which party forms the Government?

ANSWER *party with the most MP elected.*

72 What is the second largest party in the House of Commons called?

ANSWER *the opposition*

73 What type of constitution does the UK have?

ANSWER *An written constitution*

74 What is the role of the Speaker in the House of Commons?

ANSWER *To chair proceeding on the House of commons*

75 When are by-elections held?

ANSWER *to replace party MP*

76 Who is the Head of State of the United Kingdom?

ANSWER *The Queen*

77 What are the responsibilities of an MP?

ANSWER

78 What ceremonial duty does the Monarch perform in the British Parliament?

ANSWER *opening of parliament*

79 How is the Speaker of the House of Commons chosen?

ANSWER *elected by fellow MPs*

80 Who are the Whips and what do they do?

ANSWER

81 What is a Life Peer?

ANSWER

82 What are the key differences between the House of Commons and the House of Lords? *not by democratic election*

ANSWER *propose and Review the law*

83 What is the name of the system that governs how MPs are elected into the House of Commons?

ANSWER *first past the post*

84 What must a candidate achieve in order to win their constituency?

ANSWER *win the vote*

The party system

Under the British system of parliamentary democracy, anyone can stand for election as an MP but they are unlikely to win an election unless they have been nominated to represent one of the major political parties. These are the Labour Party, the Conservative Party, the Liberal Democrats, or one of the parties representing Scottish, Welsh, or Northern Irish interests. There are just a few MPs who do not represent any of the main political parties and are called 'independents'. The main political parties actively seek members among ordinary voters to join their debates, contribute to their costs, and help at elections for Parliament or for local government; they have branches in most constituencies and they hold policy-making conferences every year.

Pressure and lobby groups

Pressure and lobby groups are organisations that try to influence government policy. They play a very important role in politics. There are many pressure groups in the UK. They may represent economic interests (such as the Confederation of British Industry, the Consumers' Association, or the trade unions) or views on particular subjects (e.g. Greenpeace or Liberty). The general public is more likely to support pressure groups than join a political party.

The civil service

Civil servants are managers and administrators who carry out government policy. They have to be politically neutral and professional, regardless of which political party is in power. Although civil servants have to follow the policies of the elected government, they can warn ministers if they think a policy is impractical or not in the public interest. Before a general election takes place, top civil servants study the Opposition party's policies closely in case they need to be ready to serve a new government with different aims and policies.

Devolved administration

In order to give people in Wales and Scotland more control of matters that directly affect them, in 1997 the government began a programme of devolving power from central government. Since 1999 there has been a Welsh Assembly, a Scottish Parliament and, periodically, a Northern Ireland Assembly. Although policy and laws governing defence, foreign affairs, taxation and social security all remain under central UK government control, many other public services now come under the control of the devolved administrations in Wales and Scotland.

Both the Scottish Parliament and Welsh Assembly have been set up using forms of proportional representation which ensures that each party gets a number of seats in proportion to the number of votes they receive. Similarly, proportional representation is used in Northern Ireland in order to ensure 'power sharing' between the Unionist majority (mainly Protestant) and the substantial (mainly

Catholic) minority aligned to Irish nationalist parties. A different form of proportional representation is used for elections to the European Parliament.

The Welsh Assembly Government

The National Assembly for Wales, or Welsh Assembly Government (WAG), is situated in Cardiff, the capital city of Wales. It has 60 Assembly Members (AMs) and elections are held every four years. Members can speak in either Welsh or English and all its publications are in both languages. The Assembly has the power to make decisions on important matters such as education policy, the environment, health services, transport and local government, and to pass laws for Wales on these matters within a statutory framework set out by the UK Parliament at Westminster.

The Parliament of Scotland

A long campaign in Scotland for more independence and democratic control led to the formation in 1999 of the Parliament of Scotland, which sits in Edinburgh, the capital city of Scotland.

There are 129 Members of the Scottish Parliament (MSPs), elected by a form of proportional representation. This has led to the sharing of power in Scotland between the Labour and Liberal Democrat parties. The Scottish Parliament can pass legislation for Scotland on all matters that are not specifically reserved to the UK Parliament. The matters on which the Scottish Parliament can legislate include civil and criminal law, health, education, planning and the raising of additional taxes.

The Northern Ireland Assembly

A Northern Ireland Parliament was established in 1922 when Ireland was divided, but it was abolished in 1972 shortly after the Troubles broke out in 1969.

Soon after the end of the Troubles, the Northern Ireland Assembly was established with a power-sharing agreement which distributes ministerial offices among the main parties. The Assembly has 108 elected members known as MLAs (Members of the Legislative Assembly). Decision-making powers devolved to Northern Ireland include education, agriculture, the environment, health and social services in Northern Ireland.

The UK government kept the power to suspend the Northern Ireland Assembly if the political leaders no longer agreed to work together or if the Assembly was not working in the interests of the people of Northern Ireland. This has happened several times and the Assembly is currently suspended (2006). This means that the elected assembly members do not have power to pass bills or make decisions.

Local government

Towns, cities and rural areas in the UK are governed by democratically elected councils, often called local authorities. Some areas have both district and county councils which have different functions, although most larger towns and cities will have a single local authority. Many councils representing towns and cities appoint a mayor who is the ceremonial leader of the council but in some towns a mayor is appointed to be the effective leader of the administration. London has 33 local authorities, with the Greater London Authority and the Mayor of London co-ordinating policies across the capital. Local authorities are required to provide 'mandatory services' in their area. These services include education, housing, social services, passenger transport, the fire service, rubbish collection, planning, environmental health and libraries.

Most of the money for the local authority services comes from the government through taxes. Only about 20% is funded locally through 'council tax' a local tax set by councils to help pay for local services. It applies to all domestic properties, including houses, bungalows, flats, maisonettes, mobile homes or houseboats, whether owned or rented.

Local elections for councillors are held in May every year. Many candidates stand for council election as members of a political party.

The judiciary

In the UK the laws made by Parliament are the highest authority. But often important questions arise about how the laws are to be interpreted in particular cases. It is the task of the judges (who are together called 'the judiciary') to interpret the law, and the government may not interfere with their role. Often the actions of the government are claimed to be illegal and, if the judges agree, then the government must either change its policies or ask Parliament to change the law. This has become all the more important in recent years, as the judges now have the task of applying the Human Rights Act. If they find that a public body is not respecting a person's human rights, they may order that body to change its practices and to pay compensation, if appropriate. If the judges believe that an Act of Parliament is incompatible with the Human Rights Act, they cannot change it themselves but they can ask Parliament to consider doing so.

Judges cannot, however, decide whether people are guilty or innocent of serious crimes. When someone is accused of a serious crime, a jury will decide whether he or she is innocent or guilty and, if guilty, the judge will decide on the penalty. For less important crimes, a magistrate will decide on guilt and on any penalty.

The police

The police service is organised locally, with one police service for each county or group of counties. The largest force is the Metropolitan Police, which serves London and is based at New Scotland Yard. Northern Ireland as a whole is served by the Police Service for Northern Ireland (PSNI). The police have 'operational independence', which means that the government cannot instruct them on what to do in any particular case. But the powers of the police are limited by the law and their finances are controlled by the government and by police authorities made up of councillors and magistrates. The Independent Police Complaints Commission (or, in Northern Ireland, the Police Ombudsman) investigates serious complaints against the police.

Non-departmental public bodies (quangos)

Non-departmental public bodies, also known as quangos, are independent organisations that carry out functions on behalf of the public which it would be inappropriate to place under the political control of a Cabinet minister. There are many hundreds of these bodies, carrying out a wide variety of public duties. Appointments to these bodies are usually made by ministers, but they must do so in an open and fair way.

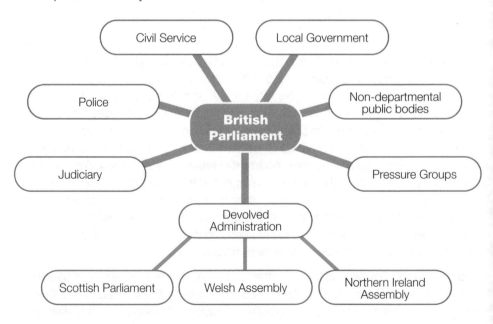

The role of the media

Proceedings in Parliament are broadcast on digital television and published in official reports such as Hansard, which is available in large libraries and on the internet: **www.parliament.uk**. Most people, however, get information about political issues and events from newspapers (often called the press), television and radio.

The UK has a free press, meaning that what is written in newspapers is free from government control. Newspaper owners and editors hold strong political opinions and run campaigns to try and influence government policy and public opinion. As a result it is sometimes difficult to distinguish fact from opinion in newspaper coverage.

By law, radio and television coverage of the political parties at election periods must be balanced and so equal time has to be given to rival viewpoints. But broadcasters are free to interview politicians in a tough and lively way.

Who can vote?

The United Kingdom has had a fully democratic system since 1928, when women were allowed to vote at 21, the same age as men. The present voting age of 18 was set in 1969, and (with a few exceptions such as convicted prisoners) all UK-born and naturalised citizens have full civic rights, including the right to vote and do jury service.

Citizens of the UK, and the Commonwealth and the Irish Republic (if resident in the UK) can vote in all public elections. Citizens of EU states who are resident in the UK can vote in all elections except national parliamentary (general) elections.

In order to vote in a parliamentary, local or European election, you must have your name on the register of electors, known as the electoral register. If you are eligible to vote, you can register by contacting your local council election registration office. If you don't know what your local authority is, you can find out by telephoning the Local Government Association (LGA) information line on 020 7664 3131 between 9am and 5pm, Monday to Friday. You will have to tell them your postcode or your full address and they will be able to give you the name of your local authority. You can also get voter registration forms in English, Welsh and some other languages on the internet: **www.electoralcommission.org.uk**

The electoral register is updated every year in September or October. An electoral registration form is sent to every household and it has to be completed and returned, with the names of everyone who is resident in the household and eligible to vote on 15 October.

In Northern Ireland a different system operates. This is called individual registration and all those entitled to vote must complete their own registration form. Once registered, you can stay on the register provided your personal details do not change. For more information telephone the Electoral Office for Northern Ireland on 028 9044 6688.

By law, each local authority has to make its electoral register available for anyone to look at, although this now has to be supervised. The register is kept at each local electoral registration office (or council office in England and Wales). It is also possible to see the register at some public buildings such as libraries.

Standing for office

Most citizens of the United Kingdom, the Irish Republic or the Commonwealth aged 18 or over can stand for public office. There are some exceptions and these include members of the armed forces, civil servants and people found guilty of certain criminal offences. Members of the House of Lords may not stand for election to the House of Commons but are eligible for all other public offices.

To become a local councillor, a candidate must have a local connection with the area through work, being on the electoral register, or through renting or owning land or property.

Contacting elected members

All elected members have a duty to serve and represent their constituents. You can get contact details for all your representatives and their parties from your local library. Assembly members, MSPs, MPs and MEPs are also listed in the phone book and Yellow Pages. You can contact MPs by letter or phone at their constituency office or their office in the House of Commons. The House of Commons, Westminster, London, SW1A 0AA, or telephone: 020 7729 3000. Many Assembly Members, MSPs, MPs and MEPs hold regular local 'surgeries'. These are often advertised in the local paper and constituents can go and talk about issues in person. You can find out the name of your local MP and get in touch with them by fax through the website: **www.writetothem.com**. This service is free.

How to visit Parliament and the Devolved Administrations

The public can listen to debates in the Palace of Westminster from public galleries in both the House of Commons and the House of Lords. You can either write to your local MP in advance to ask for tickets or you can queue on the day at the public entrance. Entrance is free. Sometimes there are long queues for the House of Commons and you may have to wait for at least one or two hours. It is usually easier to get into the House of Lords. You can find further information on the UK Parliament website: **www.parliament.uk**

In Northern Ireland, elected members, known as MLAs, meet in the Northern Ireland Assembly at Stormont, in Belfast. The Northern Ireland Assembly is presently suspended. There are two ways to arrange a visit to Stormont. You can either contact the Education Service (details on the Northern Ireland Assembly website: **www.niassembly.gov.uk**) or contact an MLA.

In Scotland, the elected members, called MSPs, meet in the Scottish Parliament at Holyrood in Edinburgh (for more information see: **www.scottish.parliament. uk**). You can get information, book tickets or arrange tours through the visitor services. You can write to them at The Scottish Parliament, Edinburgh, EH99 1SP or telephone 0131 348 5200, or email sp.bookings@scottish.parliament.uk

In Wales, the elected members, known as AMs, meet in the Welsh Assembly in the Senedd in Cardiff Bay (for more information see: **www.wales.gov.uk**). You can book guided tours or seats in the public galleries for the Welsh Assembly. To make a booking, telephone the Assembly booking line on 029 2089 8477 or email: assembly.booking@wales.gsi.gov.uk

REVISION QUESTIONS

Check your understanding of this section by completing the questions below.
Check your answers on page 194.

85 What is the name of the official reports of proceedings in Parliament?
ANSWER

86 What is another name for quangos?
ANSWER

87 How can you visit Parliament?
ANSWER

88 Where is proportional representation used in UK politics?
ANSWER

89 What are the two key features of the civil service?
ANSWER

90 How are the police structured and organised?
ANSWER

91 What responsibilities do local authorities have?
ANSWER

92 Where do local authority services get most of their funding from?
ANSWER

93 When are local government elections held?
ANSWER

94 What rights and duties do UK citizens have?
ANSWER

95 What are the basic requirements for standing for public office?
ANSWER

96 How and when do you register to vote?
ANSWER

THE UK IN EUROPE AND THE WORLD

The Commonwealth

The Commonwealth is an association of countries, most of which were once part of the British Empire, though a few countries that were not in the Empire have also joined it.

Commonwealth members

- Antigua and Barbuda
- Australia
- The Bahamas
- Bangladesh
- Barbados
- Belize
- Botswana
- Brunei Darussalam
- Cameroon
- Canada
- Cyprus
- Dominica
- Fiji Islands
- The Gambia
- Ghana
- Grenada
- Guyana
- India
- Jamaica
- Kenya
- Kiribati
- Lesotho
- Malawi
- Malaysia
- Maldives
- Malta
- Mauritius

- Mozambique
- Namibia
- Nauru*
- New Zealand
- Nigeria
- Pakistan
- Papua New Guinea
- St Kitts and Nevis
- St Lucia
- St Vincent and the Grenadines
- Samoa
- Seychelles
- Sierra Leone
- Singapore
- Solomon Islands
- South Africa
- Sri Lanka
- Swaziland
- Tonga
- Trinidad and Tobago
- Tuvalu
- Uganda
- United Kingdom
- United Republic of Tanzania
- Vanuatu
- Zambia

* Nauru is a Special Member.

The Queen is the head of the Commonwealth, which currently has 53 member states. Membership is voluntary and the Commonwealth has no power over its members although it can suspend membership. The Commonwealth aims to promote democracy, good government and to eradicate poverty.

The European Union (EU)

The European Union (EU), originally called the European Economic Community (EEC), was set up by six Western European countries who signed the Treaty of Rome on 25 March 1957. One of the main reasons for doing this was the belief that co-operation between states would reduce the likelihood of another war in Europe. Originally the UK decided not to join this group and only became part of the European Union in 1973. In 2004 ten new member countries joined the EU, with a further two in 2006 making a total of 27 member countries.

One of the main aims of the EU today is for member states to function as a single market. Most of the countries of the EU have a shared currency, the euro, but the UK has decided to retain its own currency unless the British people choose to accept the euro in a referendum. Citizens of an EU member state have the right to travel to and work in any EU country if they have a valid passport or identity card. This right can be restricted on the grounds of public health, public order and public security. The right to work is also sometimes restricted for citizens of countries that have joined the EU recently.

Institutions of the European Union

European Commission

- The civil service of the EU
- Drafts proposals for new EU policies and laws
- Administers EU funding programmes

Legislature

Council of Ministers (also known as the Council of the European Union)	**European Parliament**
• Passes EU law on the recommendations of the European Commission and the European Parliament • Takes the most important decisions about how the EU is run • Made up of government ministers from each country in the EU	• Made up of elected members (MEPs) from each country in the EU • Examines decisions made by the European Commission • Can refuse agreement to European laws proposed by the Commission • Checks on the spending of EU funds

The Council of the European Union (usually called the Council of Ministers) is effectively the governing body of the EU. It is made up of government ministers from each country in the EU and, together with the European Parliament, is the legislative body of the EU. The Council of Ministers passes EU law on the recommendations of the European Commission and the European Parliament and takes the most important decisions about how the EU is run. The European Commission is based in Brussels, the capital city of Belgium. It is the civil service of the EU and drafts proposals for new EU policies and laws and administers its funding programmes.

The European Parliament meets in Strasbourg, in north-eastern France, and in Brussels. Each country elects members, called Members of the European Parliament (MEPs), every five years. The European Parliament examines decisions made by the European Council and the European Commission, and it has the power to refuse agreement to European laws proposed by the Commission and to check on the spending of EU funds.

European Union law is legally binding in the UK and all the other member states. European laws, called directives, regulations or framework decisions, have made a lot of difference to people's rights in the UK, particularly at work. For example, there are EU directives about the procedures for making workers redundant, and regulations that limit the number of hours people can be made to work.

The Council of Europe

The Council of Europe was created in 1949 and the UK was one of the founder members. Most of the countries of Europe are members. It has no power to make laws but draws up conventions and charters which focus on human rights, democracy, education, the environment, health and culture. The most important of these is the European Convention on Human Rights; all member states are bound by this Convention and a member state which persistently refuses to obey the Convention may be expelled from the Council of Europe.

Do not confuse the Council of Europe with the Council of the European Union. The Council of Europe is a separate organisation and not a part of the executive or legislature institutions of the European Union.

The United Nations (UN)

The UK is a member of the United Nations (UN), an international organisation to which over 190 countries now belong. The UN was set up after the Second World War and aims to prevent war and promote international peace and security. There are 15 members on the UN Security Council, which recommends action by the UN when there are international crises and threats to peace. The UK is one of the five permanent members.

Three very important agreements produced by the UN are the Universal Declaration of Human Rights, the Convention on the Elimination of All Forms of Discrimination against Women, and the UN Convention on the Rights of the Child. Although none of these has the force of law, they are widely used in political debate and legal cases to reinforce the law and to assess the behaviour of countries.

REVISION QUESTIONS

Check your understanding of this section by completing the questions below.
Check your answers on page 194.

97	What is the European Commission?
	ANSWER

98	What is the main function of the Council of Europe?
	ANSWER

99	When did Britain join the European Union?
	ANSWER

100	What is one of the main aims of the European Union today?
	ANSWER

101	What is the Council of Ministers?
	ANSWER

102	Where is the European Commission based?
	ANSWER

103	What is the role of the European Parliament?
	ANSWER

104	What rights do citizens of EU member states have to travel and work in the EU?
	ANSWER

105	How many member states are there in the Commonwealth?
	ANSWER

106	What is the United Nations?
	ANSWER

107	What is the UK's role within the United Nations?
	ANSWER

CHAPTER 5: EVERYDAY NEEDS

In this chapter you will learn about some of the key services and activities integral to everyday life in Britain. Many of these services are provided by the government and others are delivered by private companies. It is important to understand the legal and other rights you have when receiving services, but also the obligations you have to meet such as taxes and other costs for services. Government services such as health care and education are delivered by various agencies, and vary between the regions of the UK. You should also focus on the detailed rules and regulations that govern many everyday activities.

Some of the information in this chapter is now out of date due to changes in law and regulations. However, only published facts, as included in this chapter, will be used for your test. Read more about this on page 207.

In this chapter there is information about:

- Housing
- Services in and for the home
- Money and credit
- Health
- Pregnancy and care of the young
- Education
- Leisure
- Travel and transport
- Identity documents

HOUSING

Buying a home

Two-thirds of people in the UK own their own home. Most other people rent houses, flats or rooms.

Mortgages

People who buy their own home usually pay for it with a mortgage, a special loan from a bank or building society. This loan is paid back, with interest, over a long period of time, usually 25 years. You can get information about mortgages from a bank or building society. Some banks can also give information about Islamic (Sharia) mortgages.

If you are having problems paying your mortgage repayments, you can get help and advice (see **Help** section later in this chapter). It is important to speak to your bank or building society as soon as you can.

Estate agents

If you wish to buy a home, usually the first place to start is an estate agent. In Scotland the process is different and you should go first to a solicitor. Estate agents represent the person selling their house or flat. They arrange for buyers to visit homes that are for sale. There are estate agents in all towns and cities and they usually have websites where they advertise the homes for sale. You can also find details about homes for sale on the internet and in national and local newspapers.

Making an offer

In the UK, except in Scotland, when you find a home you wish to buy you have to make an offer to the seller. You usually do this through an estate agent or solicitor. Many people offer a lower price than the seller is asking. Your first offer must be 'subject to contract' so that you can withdraw if there are reasons why you cannot complete the purchase. In Scotland the seller sets a price and buyers make offers over that amount. The agreement becomes legally binding earlier than it does elsewhere in the UK.

Solicitor and surveyor

It is important that a solicitor helps you through the process of buying a house or flat. When you make an offer on a property, the solicitor will carry out a number of legal checks on the property, the seller and the local area. The solicitor will provide the legal agreements necessary for you to buy the property. The bank or building society that is providing you with your mortgage will also carry out checks on the house or flat you wish to buy. These are done by a surveyor. The buyer does not usually see the result of this survey, so the buyer often asks a second surveyor to check the house as well. In Scotland the survey is carried out before an offer is made, to help people decide how much they want to bid for the property.

Rented accommodation

It is possible to rent accommodation from the local authority (the council), from a housing association or from private property owners called landlords.

The local authority

Most local authorities (or councils) provide housing. This is often called 'council housing'. In Northern Ireland social housing is provided by the Northern Ireland Housing Executive **www.nihe.co.uk**. In Scotland you can find information on social housing at **www.sfha.co.uk**. Everyone is entitled to apply for council accommodation. To apply you must put your name on the council register or list. This is available from the housing department at the local authority. You are then assessed according to your needs. This is done through a system of points. You get more points if you have priority needs, for example if you are homeless and have children or chronic ill health.

It is important to note that in many areas of the UK there is a shortage of council accommodation, and that some people have to wait a very long time for a house or flat.

Housing associations

Housing associations are independent not-for-profit organisations which provide housing for rent. In some areas they have taken over the administration of local authority housing. They also run schemes called shared ownership, which help people buy part of a house or flat if they cannot afford to buy all of it at once. There are usually waiting lists for homes owned by housing associations.

Privately rented accommodation

Many people rent houses or flats privately, from landlords. Information about private accommodation can be found in local newspapers, notice boards, estate agents and letting agents.

Tenancy agreement

When you rent a house or flat privately you sign a tenancy agreement, or lease. This explains the conditions or 'rules' you must follow while renting the property.

This agreement must be checked very carefully to avoid problems later. The agreement also contains a list of any furniture or fittings in the property. This is called an inventory. Before you sign the agreement, check the details and keep it safe during your tenancy.

Deposit and rent

You will probably be asked to give the landlord a deposit at the beginning of your tenancy. This is to cover the cost of any damage. It is usually equal to one month's rent. The landlord must return this money to you at the end of your tenancy, unless you have caused damage to the property.

Your rent is fixed with your landlord at the beginning of the tenancy. The landlord cannot raise the rent without your agreement.

If you have a low income or are unemployed you may be able to claim Housing Benefit (see Help) to help you pay your rent.

Renewing and ending a tenancy

Your tenancy agreement will be for a fixed period of time, often six months. After this time the tenancy can be ended or, if both tenant and landlord agree, renewed. If you end the tenancy before the fixed time, you usually have to pay the rent for the agreed full period of the tenancy.

A landlord cannot force a tenant to leave. If a landlord wishes a tenant to leave they must follow the correct procedures. These vary according to the type of tenancy. It is a criminal offence for a landlord to use threats or violence against a tenant or to force them to leave without an order from court.

Discrimination

It is unlawful for a landlord to discriminate against someone looking for accommodation because of their sex, race, nationality, or ethnic group, or because they are disabled, unless the landlord or a close relative of the landlord is sharing the accommodation.

Homelessness

If you are homeless you should go for help to the local authority (or, in Northern Ireland, the Housing Executive). They have a legal duty to offer help and advice, but will not offer you a place to live unless you have priority need (see above) and have a connection with the area, such as work or family. You must also show that you have not made yourself intentionally homeless.

Help

If you are homeless or have problems with your landlord, help can be found from the following:

● The housing department of the local authority will give advice on homelessness and on Housing Benefit as well as deal with problems you may have in council-owned property

● The Citizens Advice Bureau will give advice on all types of housing problems. There may also be a housing advice centre in your neighbourhood

● Shelter is a housing charity which runs a 24-hour helpline on 0808 800 4444, or visit **www.shelternet.org.uk**

● Help with the cost of moving and setting up home may be available from the Social Fund. This is run by the Department for Work and Pensions (DWP). It provides grants and loans such as the Community Care Grant for people setting up home after being homeless or after they have been in prison or other institutions. Other loans are available for people who have had an emergency such as flooding. Information about these is available at the Citizens Advice Bureau or Jobcentre Plus.

REVISION QUESTIONS

Check your understanding of this section by completing the questions below. Check your answers on page 195.

108 What is the role of an estate agent?

ANSWER

109 Where can you get help if you are homeless?

ANSWER

110 What role does a surveyor perform when you are buying a house?

ANSWER

111 What proportion of people in the UK own their own home?

ANSWER

112 How do you apply for council accommodation?

ANSWER

113 Why would you pay a deposit when you rent a home?

ANSWER

SERVICES IN AND FOR THE HOME

Water

Water is supplied to all homes in the UK. The charge for this is called the water rates. When you move in to a new home (bought or rented), you should receive a letter telling you the name of the company responsible for supplying your water. The water rates may be paid in one payment (a lump sum) or in instalments, usually monthly. If you receive Housing Benefit, you should check to see if this covers the water rates. The cost of the water usually depends on the size of your property, but some homes have a water meter which tells you exactly how much water you have used. In Northern Ireland water is currently (2006) included in the domestic rates (see **Council Tax**), although this may change in future.

Electricity and gas

All properties in the UK have electricity supplied at 240 volts. Most homes also have gas. When you move into a new home or leave an old one, you should make a note of the electricity and gas meter readings. If you have an urgent problem with your gas, electricity or water supply, you can ring a 24-hour helpline. This can be found on your bill, in the Yellow Pages or in the phone book.

Gas and electricity suppliers

It is possible to choose between different gas and electricity suppliers. These have different prices and different terms and conditions. Get advice before you sign a contract with a new supplier. To find out which company supplies your gas, telephone Transco on 0870 608 1524.

To find out which company supplies your electricity, telephone Energywatch on 0845 906 0708 or visit: **www.energywatch.org.uk**. Energywatch can also give you advice on changing your supplier of electricity or gas.

Telephone

Most homes already have a telephone line (called a land line). If you need a new line, telephone BT on 150 442, or contact a cable company. Many companies offer land line, mobile telephone and broadband internet services. You can get advice about prices or about changing your company from Ofcom at: **www.ofcom.org.uk**. You can call from public payphones using cash, pre-paid phonecards or credit or debit cards. Calls made from hotels and hostels are usually more expensive. Dial 999 or 112 for emergency calls for police, fire or ambulance services. These calls are free. Do not use these numbers if it is not a real emergency; you can always find the local numbers for these services in the phone book.

Bills

Information on how to pay for water, gas, electricity and the telephone is found on the back of each bill. If you have a bank account you can pay your bills by standing order or direct debit. Most companies operate a budget scheme which allows you to pay a fixed sum every month. If you do not pay a bill, the service can be cut off. To get a service reconnected, you have to pay another charge.

Refuse collection

Refuse is also called waste, or rubbish. The local authority collects the waste regularly, usually on the same day of each week. Waste must be put outside in a particular place to get collected. In some parts of the country the waste is put into plastic bags, in others it is put into bins with wheels. In many places you must recycle your rubbish, separating paper, glass, metal or plastic from the other rubbish. Large objects which you want to throw away, such as a bed, a wardrobe or a fridge, need to be collected separately. Contact the local authority to arrange this. If you have a business, such as a factory or a shop, you must make special arrangements with the local authority for your waste to be collected. It is a criminal offence to dump rubbish anywhere.

Council Tax

Local government services, such as education, police, roads, refuse collection and libraries, are paid for partly by grants from the government and partly by Council Tax (see chapter 4 – **Local Government**). In Northern Ireland there is a system of domestic rates instead of the Council Tax. The amount of Council Tax you pay depends on the size and value of your house or flat (dwelling). You must register to pay Council Tax when you move into a new property, either as the owner or the tenant. You can pay the tax in one payment, in two instalments, or in ten instalments (from April to January).

If only one person lives in the flat or house, you get a 25% reduction on your Council Tax. (This does not apply in Northern Ireland.) You may also get a reduction if someone in the property has a disability. People on a low income or who receive benefits such as Income Support or Jobseeker's Allowance can get Council Tax Benefit. You can get advice on this from the local authority or the Citizens Advice Bureau.

Buildings and household insurance

If you buy a home with a mortgage, you must insure the building against fire, theft and accidental damage. The landlord should arrange insurance for rented buildings. It is also wise to insure your possessions against theft or damage. There are many companies that provide insurance.

Neighbours

If you live in rented accommodation, you will have a tenancy agreement. This explains all the conditions of your tenancy. It will probably include information on what to do if you have problems with your housing. Occasionally, there may be problems with your neighbours. If you do have problems with your neighbours, they can usually be solved by speaking to them first. If you cannot solve the problem, speak to your landlord, local authority or housing association. Keep a record of the problems in case you have to show exactly what the problems are and when they started. Neighbours who cause a very serious nuisance may be taken to court and can be evicted from their home.

There are several mediation organisations which help neighbours to solve their disputes without having to go to court. Mediators talk to both sides and try to find a solution acceptable to both. You can get details of mediation organisations from the local authority, Citizens Advice, and Mediation UK on 0117 904 6661 or visit: **www.mediationuk.co.uk**

REVISION QUESTIONS

Check your understanding of this section by completing the questions below. Check your answers on page 195.

114	What services are funded by Council Tax?
	ANSWER

115	What should you do if you have problems with your neighbours?
	ANSWER

116	Describe the two ways in which water rates can be calculated
	ANSWER

117	What organisation is responsible for collecting refuse?
	ANSWER

118	If you buy a home with a mortgage, what risks must you insure the building against?
	ANSWER

MONEY AND CREDIT

Bank notes in the UK come in denominations (values) of £5, £10, £20 and £50. Northern Ireland and Scotland have their own bank notes which are valid everywhere in the UK, though sometimes people may not realise this and may not wish to accept them.

The euro

In January 2002 twelve European Union (EU) states adopted the euro as their common currency. The UK government decided not to adopt the euro at that time, and has said it will only do so if the British people vote for the euro in a referendum. The euro does circulate to some extent in Northern Ireland, particularly in the towns near the border with Ireland.

Foreign currency

You can get or change foreign currency at banks, building societies, large post offices and exchange shops or bureaux de change. You might have to order some currencies in advance. The exchange rates vary and you should check for the best deal.

Banks and building societies

Most adults in the UK have a bank or building society account. Many large national banks or building societies have branches in towns and cities throughout the UK. It is worth checking the different types of account each one offers. Many employers pay salaries directly into a bank or building society account. There are many banks and building societies to choose from. To open an account, you need to show documents to prove your identity, such as a passport, immigration document or driving licence. You also need to show something with your address on it like a tenancy agreement or household bill. It is also possible to open bank accounts in some supermarkets or on the internet.

Cash and debit cards

Cash cards allow you to use cash machines to withdraw money from your account. For this you need a Personal Identification Number (PIN) which you must keep secret. A debit card allows you to pay for things without using cash. You must have enough money in your account to cover what you buy. If you lose your cash card or debit card you must inform the bank immediately.

Credit and store cards

Credit cards can be used to buy things in shops, on the telephone and over the internet. A store card is like a credit card but used only in a specific shop. Credit and store cards do not draw money from your bank account, but you will be sent a bill every month. If you do not pay the total amount on the bill, you are charged interest. Although credit and store cards are useful, the interest is usually very high and many people fall into debt this way. If you lose your credit or store cards you must inform the company immediately.

Credit and loans

People in the UK often borrow money from banks and other organisations to pay for things like household goods, cars and holidays. This is more common in the UK than in many other countries. You must be very sure of the terms and conditions when you decide to take out a loan. You can get advice on loans from the Citizens Advice Bureau if you are uncertain.

Being refused credit

Banks and other organisations use different information about you to make a decision about a loan, such as your occupation, address, salary and previous credit record. If you apply for a loan you might be refused. If this happens, you have the right to ask the reason why.

Credit unions

Credit unions are financial co-operatives owned and controlled by their members. The members pool their savings and then make loans from this pool. Interest rates in credit unions are usually lower than banks and building societies. There are credit unions in many cities and towns. To find the nearest credit union contact the Association of British Credit Unions (ABCUL) on: **www.abcul.coop**

Insurance

As well as insuring their property and possessions (see above), many people insure their credit cards and mobile phones. They also buy insurance when they travel abroad in case they lose their luggage or need medical treatment. Insurance is compulsory if you have a car or motorcycle. You can usually arrange insurance directly with an insurance company, or you can use a broker who will help you get the best deal.

Social security

The UK has a system of social security which pays welfare benefits to people who do not have enough money to live on. Benefits are usually available for the sick and disabled, older people, the unemployed and those on low incomes. People who do not have legal rights of residence (or 'settlement') in the UK cannot usually receive benefits. Arrangements for paying and receiving benefits are complex because they have to cover people in many different situations. Guides to benefits are available from Jobcentre Plus offices, local libraries, post offices and the Citizens Advice Bureau.

REVISION QUESTIONS

Check your understanding of this section by completing the questions below. Check your answers on page 195.

119 What do you need to open a bank or building society account?

ANSWER

120 What is the difference between debit, credit and store cards?

ANSWER

121	What are credit unions?
	ANSWER

122	Where can you go to get information on social security benefits?
	ANSWER

123	Where can you go to get help if you have problems with debt?
	ANSWER

124	What denominations do bank notes in the UK come in?
	ANSWER

HEALTH

Healthcare in the UK is organised under the National Health Service (NHS). The NHS began in 1948, and is one of the largest organisations in Europe. It provides all residents with free healthcare and treatment.

Finding a doctor

Family doctors are called General Practitioners (GPs) and they work in surgeries. GPs often work together in a group practice. This is sometimes called a Primary Health Care Centre.

Your GP is responsible for organising the health treatment you receive. Treatment can be for physical and mental illnesses. If you need to see a specialist, you must go to your GP first. Your GP will then refer you to a specialist in a hospital. Your GP can also refer you for specialist treatment if you have special needs.

You can get a list of local GPs from libraries, post offices, the tourist information office, the Citizens Advice Bureau, the local Health Authority and from the following websites:

www.nhs.uk for health practitioners in England;
www.wales.nhs.uk/directory.cfm for health practitioners in Wales;
www.n-i.nhs.uk for health practitioners in Northern Ireland;
www.show.scot.nhs.uk/findnearest/healthservices in Scotland.

You can also ask neighbours and friends for the name of their local doctor.

You can attend a hospital without a GP's letter only in the case of an emergency.

If you have an emergency you should go to the Accident and Emergency (A & E) department of the nearest hospital.

Registering with a GP

You should look for a GP as soon as you move to a new area. You should not wait until you are ill. The health centre, or surgery, will tell you what you need to do to register. Usually you must have a medical card. If you do not have one, the GP's receptionist should give you a form to send to the local health authority. They will then send you a medical card.

Before you register you should check the surgery can offer what you need. For example, you might need a woman GP, or maternity services. Sometimes GPs have many patients and are unable to accept new ones. If you cannot find a GP, you can ask your local health authority to help you find one.

Using your doctor

All patients registering with a GP are entitled to a free health check. Appointments to see the GP can be made by phone or in person. Sometimes you might have to wait several days before you can see a doctor. If you need immediate medical attention ask for an urgent appointment. You should go to the GP's surgery a few minutes before the appointment. If you cannot attend or do not need the appointment any more, you must let the surgery know. The GP needs patients to answer all questions as fully as possible in order to find out what is wrong. Everything you tell the GP is completely confidential and cannot be passed on to anyone else without your permission. If you do not understand something, ask for clarification. If you have difficulties with English, bring someone who can help you, or ask the receptionist for an interpreter. This must be done when you make the appointment. If you have asked for an interpreter, it is important that you keep your appointment because this service is expensive.

In exceptional circumstances, GPs can visit patients at home but they always give priority to people who are unable to travel. If you call the GP outside normal working hours, you will have to answer several questions about your situation. This is to assess how serious your case is. You will then be told if a doctor can come to your home. You might be advised to go to the nearest A & E department.

Charges

Treatment from the GP is free but you have to pay a charge for your medicines and for certain services, such as vaccinations for travel abroad. If the GP decides you need to take medicine you will be given a prescription. You must take this to a pharmacy (chemist).

Prescriptions

Prescriptions are free for anyone who is

● under 16 years of age (under 25 in Wales)

● under 19 and in full-time education

● aged 60 or over

● pregnant or with a baby under 12 months old

● suffering from a specified medical condition

● receiving Income Support, Jobseeker's Allowance, Working Families or Disabilities Tax Credit.

Feeling unwell

If you or your child feels unwell you have the following options:

For information or advice

● ask your local pharmacist (chemist). The pharmacy can give advice on medicines and some illnesses and conditions that are not serious

● speak to a nurse by phoning NHS Direct on 0845 46 47

● use the NHS Direct website, NHS Direct Online: **www.nhsdirect.nhs.uk**

To see a doctor or nurse

● make an appointment to see your GP or a nurse working in the surgery

● visit an NHS walk-in centre.

For urgent medical treatment

● contact your GP

● go to your nearest hospital with an Accident and Emergency department

● call 999 for an ambulance. Calls are free. ONLY use this service for a real emergency.

NHS Direct is a 24-hour telephone service which provides information on particular health conditions. Telephone: 0845 46 47. You may ask for an interpreter for advice in your own language. In Scotland, NHS24 at: **www.nhs24.com** telephone 08454 24 24 24.

NHS Direct Online is a website providing information about health services and several medical conditions and treatments: **www.nhsdirect.nhs.uk**

NHS walk-in centres provide treatment for minor injuries and illnesses seven days a week. You do not need an appointment. For details of your nearest centre call NHS Direct or visit the NHS website at: **www.nhs.uk** (for Northern Ireland **www.n-i.nhs.uk**) and click on 'local NHS services'.

Going into hospital

If you need minor tests at a hospital, you will probably attend the Outpatients department. If your treatment takes several hours, you will go into hospital as a day patient. If you need to stay overnight, you will go into hospital as an in-patient.

You should take personal belongings with you, such as a towel, night clothes, things for washing, and a dressing gown. You will receive all your meals while you are an in-patient. If you need advice about going into hospital, contact Customer Services or the Patient Advice and Liaison Service (PALS) at the hospital where you will receive treatment.

Dentists

You can get the name of a dentist by asking at the local library, at the Citizens Advice Bureau and through NHS Direct. Most people have to pay for dental treatment. Some dentists work for the NHS and some are private. NHS dentists charge less than private dentists, but some dentists have two sets of charges, both NHS and private. A dentist should explain your treatment and the charges before the treatment begins.

Free dental treatment is available to

● people under 18 (in Wales people under 25 and over 60)

● pregnant women and women with babies under 12 months old

● people on income support, Jobseeker's Allowance or Pension Credit Guarantee.

Opticians

Most people have to pay for sight tests and glasses, except children, people over

60, people with certain eye conditions and people receiving certain benefits. In Scotland, eye tests are free.

Pregnancy and care of young children

If you are pregnant you will receive regular ante-natal care. This is available from your local hospital, local health centre or from special ante-natal clinics. You will receive support from a GP and from a midwife. Midwives work in hospitals or health centres. Some GPs do not provide maternity services so you may wish to look for another GP during your pregnancy. In the UK women usually have their babies in hospital, especially if it is their first baby. It is common for the father to attend the birth, but only if the mother wants him to be there.

A short time after you have your child, you will begin regular contact with a health visitor. She or he is a qualified nurse and can advise you about caring for your baby. The first visits will be in your home, but after that you might meet the health visitor at a clinic. You can ask advice from your health visitor until your child is five years old. In most towns and cities there are mother and toddler groups or playgroups for small children. These often take place at local churches and community centres. You might be able to send your child to a nursery school (see **Going to school**).

Information on pregnancy

You can get information on maternity and ante-natal services in your area from your local health authority, a health visitor or your GP. The number of your health authority will be in the phone book.

The Family Planning Association (FPA) gives advice on contraception and sexual health. The FPA's helpline is 0845 310 1334, or: **www.fpa.org.uk**

The National Childbirth Trust gives information and support in pregnancy, childbirth and early parenthood: **www.nctpregnancyandbabycare.com**

Registering a birth

You must register your baby with the Registrar of Births, Marriages and Deaths (Register Office) within six weeks of the birth. The address of your local Register Office is in the phone book. If the parents are married, either the mother or father can register the birth. If they are not married, only the mother can register the birth. If the parents are not married but want both names on the child's birth certificate, both mother and father must be present when they register their baby.

REVISION QUESTIONS

Check your understanding of this section by completing the questions below.
Check your answers on page 196.

125 How can you find and register with a GP?

ANSWER

126 How can you find a dentist?

ANSWER

127 When should you attend A&E?

ANSWER

128 When should you phone 999 or 112?

ANSWER

129 What service is available from NHS Direct?

ANSWER

130 Where can you go to get health advice and treatment while you are pregnant?

ANSWER

131 Where and when must you register the birth of your baby?

ANSWER

EDUCATION

Going to school

Education in the UK is free and compulsory for all children between the ages of 5 and 16 (4 to 16 in Northern Ireland). The education system varies in England, Scotland, Wales and Northern Ireland.

The child's parent or guardian is responsible for making sure their child goes to school, arrives on time and attends for the whole school year. If they do not do this, the parent or guardian may be prosecuted.

Some areas of the country offer free nursery education for children over the age of 3. In most parts of the UK, compulsory education is divided into two stages, primary and secondary. In some places there is a middle-school system. In England and Wales the primary stage lasts from 5 to 11, in Scotland from 5 to 12 and in Northern Ireland from 4 to 11. The secondary stage lasts until the age of 16. At that age young people can choose to leave school or to continue with their education until they are 17 or 18.

Details of local schools are available from your local education authority office or website. The addresses and phone numbers of local education authorities are in the phone book.

Primary schools

These are usually schools where both boys and girls learn together and are usually close to a child's home. Children tend to be with the same group and teacher all day. Schools encourage parents to help their children with learning, particularly with reading and writing.

Secondary schools

At age 11 (12 in Scotland) children go to secondary school. This might normally be the school nearest their home, but parents in England and Wales are allowed to express a preference for a different school. In some areas, getting a secondary school place in a preferred school can be difficult, and parents often apply to several schools in order to make sure their child gets offered a place. In Northern Ireland many schools select children through a test taken at the age of 11.

If the preferred school has enough places, the child will be offered a place. If there are not enough places, children will be offered places according to the school's admission arrangements. Admission arrangements vary from area to area.

Secondary schools are larger than primary schools. Most are mixed sex, although there are single sex schools in some areas. Your local education authority will give you information on schools in your area. It will also tell you which schools have spaces and give you information about why some children will be given places when only a few are available and why other children might not. It will also tell you how to apply for a secondary school place.

Costs

Education at state schools in the UK is free, but parents have to pay for school uniforms and sports wear. There are sometimes extra charges for music lessons and for school outings. Parents on low incomes can get help with costs, and with the cost of school meals. You can get advice on this from the local education authority or the Citizens Advice Bureau.

Church and other faith schools

Some primary and secondary schools in the UK are linked to the Church of England or the Roman Catholic Church. These are called 'faith schools'. In some areas there are Muslim, Jewish and Sikh schools. In Northern Ireland, some schools are called Integrated Schools. These schools aim to bring children of different religions together. Information on faith schools is available from your local education authority.

Independent schools

Independent schools are private schools. They are not run or paid for by the state. Independent secondary schools are also sometimes called public schools. There are about 2,500 independent schools in the UK. About 8% of children go to these schools. At independent schools parents must pay the full cost of their child's education. Some independent schools offer scholarships which pay some or all of the costs of the child's education.

The school curriculum

All state, primary and secondary schools in England, Wales and Northern Ireland follow the National Curriculum. This covers English, maths, science, design and technology, information and communication technology (ICT), history, geography, modern foreign languages, art and design, music, physical education (PE) and citizenship. In Wales, children learn Welsh.

In some primary schools in Wales, all the lessons are taught in Welsh. In Scotland, pupils follow a broad curriculum informed by national guidance. Schools must, by law, provide religious education (RE) to all pupils. Parents are allowed to withdraw their children from these lessons. RE lessons have a Christian basis but children also learn about the other major religions.

Assessment

In England, the curriculum is divided into four stages, called Key Stages. After each stage children are tested. They take Key Stage tests (also called SATs) at ages 7, 11 and 14. At 16 they usually take the General Certificates of Secondary Education (GCSEs) in several subjects, although some schools also offer other qualifications. At 18, young people who have stayed at school do AGCEs (Advanced GCE levels) often just called A levels.

In Wales, schools follow the Welsh National Curriculum but have abolished national tests for children at age 7 and 11. There are also plans in Wales to stop testing children at 14. Teachers in Wales still have to assess and report on their pupils' progress and achievements at 7 and 11.

In Scotland, the curriculum is divided into two phases. The first phase is from 5 to 14. There are six levels in this phase, levels A to F. There are no tests for whole groups during this time. Teachers test individual children when they are ready. From 14 to 16, young people do Standard Grade. After 16 they can study at Intermediate, Higher or Advanced level. In Scotland there will soon be a single curriculum for all pupils from age 3 to age 18. This is called 'A Curriculum for Excellence'. More information can be found at:
www.acurriculumforexcellencescotland.gov.uk

Help with English

If your child's main language is not English, the school may arrange for extra language support from an EAL (English Additional Language) specialist teacher.

Careers education

All children get careers advice from the age of 14. Advice is also available from Connexions, a national service for young people: telephone 080 800 13219 or: **www.connexions-direct.com** in England. In Wales, Careers Wales offers advice to children from the age of 11. For further information visit: **www.careerswales. com** or telephone 0800 100 900.

In Scotland, Careers Scotland provides information, services and support to all ages and stages. For further information visit: **www.careers-scotland.org.uk** or telephone 0845 8 502 502.

Parents and schools

Many parents are involved with their child's school. A number of places on a school's governing body are reserved for parents. The governing body decides how the school is run and administered and produces reports on the progress of the school from year to year. In Scotland, parents can be members of school boards or parent councils.

Schools must be open 190 days a year. Term dates are decided by the governing body or by the local education authority. Children must attend the whole school year. Schools expect parents and guardians to inform them if their child is going to be absent from school. All schools ask parents to sign a home-school agreement. This is a list of things that both the school and the parent or guardian agree to do to ensure a good education for the child. All parents receive a report every year on their child's progress. They also have the chance to go to the school to talk to their child's teachers.

Further education and adult education

At 16, young people can leave school or stay on to do A levels (Higher grades in Scotland) in preparation for university. Some young people go to their local further education (FE) college to improve their exam grades or to get new qualifications for a career. Most courses are free up to the age of 19. Young people from families with low incomes can get financial help with their studies when they leave school at 16. This is called the Education Maintenance Allowance (EMA). Information about this is available at your local college or at: **www.dfes.gov.uk**

Further education colleges also offer courses to adults over the age of 18. These include courses for people wishing to improve their skills in English. These courses are called ESOL (English for Speakers of Other Languages). There are also courses for English speakers who need to improve their literacy and numeracy and for people who need to learn new skills for employment. ESOL courses are also available in community centres and training centres. There is sometimes a waiting list for ESOL courses because demand is high. In England and Wales, ESOL, literacy and numeracy courses are also called Skills for Life courses. You can get information at your local college or local library or from Learndirect on 0800 100 900.

Many people join other adult education classes to learn a new skill or hobby and to meet new people. Classes are very varied and range from sports to learning a musical instrument or a new language. Details are usually available from your local library, college or adult education centre.

University

More young people go to university now than in the past. Many go after A levels (or Higher grades in Scotland) at age 18 but it is also possible to go to university later in life. At present, most students in England, Wales and Northern Ireland have to pay towards the cost of their tuition fees and to pay for their living expenses. In Scotland there are no tuition fees but after students finish university they pay back some of the cost of their education in a payment called an endowment. At present, universities can charge up to £3,000 per year for their tuition fees, but students do not have to pay anything towards their fees before or during their studies. The government pays their tuition fees and then charges for them when a student starts working after university. Some families on low incomes receive help with their children's tuition fees. This is called a grant. The universities also give help, in the form of bursaries. Most students get a low-interest student loan from a bank. This pays for their living costs while they are at university. When a student finishes university and starts working, he or she must pay back the loan.

REVISION QUESTIONS

Check your understanding of this section by completing the questions below.
Check your answers on page 196.

132	What are the different stages of a child's education through the schooling system?
	ANSWER

133	What are the differences between a state school, faith school, integrated school and independent school?
	ANSWER

134	What is the National Curriculum?
	ANSWER

135	What is the role of the governing body of a school?
	ANSWER

136	What are some of the courses available at Further Education colleges?
	ANSWER

LEISURE

Information

Information about theatre, cinema, music and exhibitions is found in local newspapers, local libraries and tourist information offices. Many museums and art galleries are free.

Film, video and DVD

Films in the UK have a system to show if they are suitable for children. This is called the classification system. If a child is below the age of the classification, they should not watch the film at a cinema or on DVD. All films receive a classification, as follows:

U (Universal): Suitable for anyone aged 4 years and over

 PG (Parental Guidance): Suitable for everyone but some parts of the film might be unsuitable for children. Their parents should decide

 12 or 12A: Children under 12 are not allowed to see or rent the film unless they are with an adult

 15: Children under 15 are not allowed to see or rent the film

 18: No one under 18 is allowed to see or rent the film

 R18: No one under 18 is allowed to see the film, which is only available in specially licensed cinemas

Television and radio

Anyone in the UK with a television (TV), DVD or video recorder, computer or any device which is used for watching or recording TV programmes must be covered by a valid television licence. One licence covers all of the equipment at one address, but people who rent different rooms in a shared house must each buy a separate licence.

A colour TV licence currently costs £131.50 (2006) and lasts for 12 months. People aged 75, or over can apply for a free TV licence. Blind people can claim a 50% discount on their TV licence. You risk prosecution and a fine if you watch TV but are not covered by a TV licence. There are many ways to buy a TV licence including from local Pay Point outlets or on-line at: **www.tvlicensing.co.uk**. It is also possible to pay for the licence in instalments. For more information telephone 0870 576 3763 or write to TV Licensing, Bristol, BS98 1TL.

Sports, clubs and societies

Information about local clubs and societies can usually be found at local libraries or through your local authority. For information about sports you should ask in the local leisure centre. Libraries and leisure centres often organise activities for children during the school holidays.

Places of interest

The UK has a large network of public footpaths in the countryside. Many parts of the countryside and places of interest are kept open by the National Trust. This is a charity that works to preserve important buildings and countryside in the UK. Information about National Trust buildings and areas open to the public is available on: **www.nationaltrust.org.uk**

Pubs and night clubs

Public houses, or pubs, are an important part of social life in the UK. To drink alcohol in a pub you must be 18 or over. People under 18 are not allowed to buy alcohol in a supermarket or in an off-licence either. The landlord of the pub may allow people of 14 to come into the pub but they are not allowed to drink. At 16, people can drink wine or beer with a meal in a hotel or restaurant.

Allowed to drink alcohol in a pub	Allowed to drink wine or beer with a meal in a hotel or restaurant	May be allowed into a pub, but not allowed to drink

Pubs are usually open during the day and until 11pm. If a pub wants to stay open later, it must apply for a special licence. Night clubs open and close later than pubs.

Betting and gambling

People under 18 are not allowed into betting shops or gambling clubs. There is a National Lottery for which draws, with large prizes, are made every week. You can enter by buying a ticket or a scratch card. People under 16 are not allowed to buy a lottery ticket or scratch card.

Pets

Many people in the UK have pets such as cats and dogs. It is against the law to treat a pet cruelly or to neglect it. All dogs in public places must wear a collar showing the name and address of the owner. The owner is responsible for keeping the dog under control and for cleaning up after the animal in a public place. Vaccinations and medical treatment for animals are available from veterinary surgeons (vets). If you cannot afford to pay a vet, you can go to a charity called the PDSA (People's Dispensary for Sick Animals). To find your nearest branch, visit: **www.pdsa.org.uk**

REVISION QUESTIONS

Check your understanding of this section by completing the questions below. Check your answers on page 197.

137 How are films classified?

ANSWER

138 Who must buy a television licence?

ANSWER

139 What are the laws about the selling and drinking of alcohol?

ANSWER

140 What is the National Trust?

ANSWER

TRAVEL AND TRANSPORT

Trains, buses and coaches

For information about trains telephone the National Rail Enquiry Service: 08457 48 49 50, or visit: **www.nationalrail.co.uk**. For trains in Northern Ireland, phone Translink on 028 90 66 66 30 or visit: **www.translink.co.uk**. For information about local bus times phone 0870 608 250. For information on coaches, telephone National Express on 08705 80 80 80, or visit: **www.nationalexpress.com**.

For coaches in Scotland, telephone Scottish Citylink on 08705 50 50 50 or visit: **www.citylink.co.uk**. For Northern Ireland, visit: **www.translink.co.uk**

Usually, tickets for trains and underground systems such as the London Underground must be bought before you get on the train. The fare varies according to the day and time you wish to travel. Travelling in the rush hour is always more expensive. Discount tickets are available for families, people aged 60 and over, disabled people, students and people under 26. Ask at your local train station for details. Failure to buy a ticket may result in a penalty.

Taxis

To operate legally, all taxis and minicabs must be licensed and display a licence plate. Taxis and cabs with no licence are not insured for fare-paying passengers and are not always safe. Women should not use unlicensed minicabs.

Driving

You must be at least 17 to drive a car or motorcycle, 18 to drive a medium-sized lorry, and 21 to drive a large lorry or bus. To drive a lorry, minibus or bus with more than eight passenger seats, you must have a special licence.

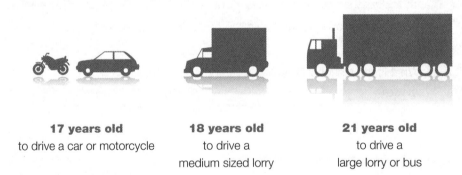

17 years old	**18 years old**	**21 years old**
to drive a car or motorcycle	to drive a medium sized lorry	to drive a large lorry or bus

The driving licence

You must have a driving licence to drive on public roads. To get a driving licence you must pass a test. There are many driving schools where you can learn with the help of a qualified instructor.

You get a full driving licence in three stages:

1. Apply for a provisional licence. You need this licence while you are learning to

drive. With this you are allowed to drive a motorcycle up to 125cc or a car. You must put L plates on the vehicle, or D plates in Wales. Learner drivers cannot drive on a motorway. If you drive a car, you must be with someone who is over 21 and who has had a full licence for over three years. You can get an application form for a provisional licence from a post office.

2. Pass a written theory test.

3. Pass a practical driving test.

Drivers may use their licence until they are 70. After that the licence is valid for three years at a time.

In Northern Ireland, a newly-qualified driver must display an R-Plate (for registered driver) for one year after passing the test.

Overseas licences

If your driving licence is from a country in the European Union (EU), Iceland, Liechtenstein or Norway, you can drive in the UK for as long as your licence is valid.

If you have a licence from a country outside the EU, you may use it in the UK for up to 12 months. During this time you must get a UK provisional driving licence and pass both the UK theory and practical driving tests, or you will not be able to drive after 12 months.

Insurance

It is a criminal offence to have a car without proper motor insurance. Drivers without insurance can receive very high fines. It is also illegal to allow someone to use your car if they are not insured to drive it.

Road tax and MOT

You must also pay a tax to drive your car on the roads. This is called road tax. Your vehicle must have a road tax disc which shows you have paid. You can buy this at the post office. If you do not pay the road tax, your vehicle may be clamped or towed away.

If your vehicle is over three years old, you must take it every year for a Ministry of Transport (MOT) test. You can do this at an approved garage. The garage will give you an MOT certificate when your car passes the test. It is an offence not to have an MOT certificate. If you do not have an MOT certificate, your insurance will not be valid.

Safety

Everyone in a vehicle should wear a seat belt. Children under 12 years of age may need a special booster seat. Motorcyclists and their passengers must wear a crash helmet (this law does not apply to Sikh men if they are wearing a turban). It is illegal to drive while holding a mobile phone.

Speed limits

For cars and motorcycles the speed limits are:

- 30 miles per hour (mph) in built-up areas, unless a sign shows a different limit
- 60 mph on single carriageways
- 70 mph on motorways and dual carriageways

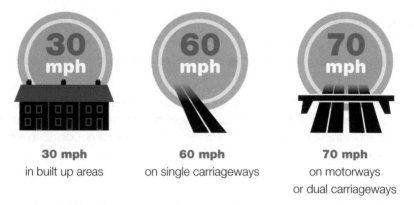

30 mph	**60 mph**	**70 mph**
in built up areas	on single carriageways	on motorways
		or dual carriageways

Speed limits are lower for buses, lorries and cars pulling caravans.

It is illegal to drive when you are over the alcohol limit or drunk. The police can stop you and give you a test to see how much alcohol you have in your body. This is called a breathalyser test. If a driver has more than the permitted amount of alcohol (called being 'over the limit') or refuses to take the test, he or she will be arrested. People who drink and drive can expect to be disqualified from driving for a long period.

Accidents

If you are involved in a road accident:

- don't drive away without stopping – this is a criminal offence
- call the police and ambulance on 999 or 112 if someone is injured

● get the names, addresses, vehicle registration numbers and insurance details of the other drivers

● give your details to the other drivers or passengers and to the police

● make a note of everything that happened and contact your insurance company as soon as possible.

Note that if you admit the accident was your fault, the insurance company may refuse to pay. It is better to wait until the insurance company decides for itself whose fault the accident was.

Identity documents

At present, UK citizens do not have to carry identity (ID) cards. The government is, however, making plans to introduce them in the next few years.

Proving your identity

You may have to prove your identity at different times, such as when you open a bank account, rent accommodation, enrol for a college course, hire a car, apply for benefits such as housing benefit, or apply for a marriage certificate. Different organisations may ask for different documents as proof of identity. These can include:

● official documents from the Home Office showing your immigration status

● a certificate of identity

● a passport or travel document

● a National Insurance (NI) number card

● a provisional or full driving licence

● a recent gas, electricity or phone bill showing your name and address

● a rent or benefits book.

REVISION QUESTIONS

Check your understanding of this section by completing the questions below.
Check your answers on page 197.

141	How can you get a driving licence?
	ANSWER

142	What do you require to be allowed to drive a vehicle in the UK?
	ANSWER

143	What should you do if you have a car accident?
	ANSWER

144	When might you have to prove your identity?
	ANSWER

145	How can you prove your identity?
	ANSWER

146	What are the three main speed limits for cars and motorcycles on UK roads?
	ANSWER

CHAPTER 6: EMPLOYMENT

In this chapter you will learn about working in Britain. Much of what you need to learn relates to your rights and responsibilities as an employee. As an employee you should always be treated fairly in terms of pay, health and safety and access to opportunities. At the same time you must also behave honestly and meet your obligations such as tax and National Insurance. You also have to understand the rules and rights for families in relation to employment. This includes both the rights that parents have to spend time with their children but also the strict limitations that are in place to ensure that children are not exploited in the work place, so that they are able to pursue their education without interference.

Some of the information in this chapter is now out of date due to changes in law and regulations. However, only published facts, as included in this chapter, will be used for your test. Read more about this on page 207.

In this chapter there is information about:

● Looking for work and applying for jobs

● Training and volunteering

● Equal rights and discrimination

● Rights and responsibilities at work

● Working for yourself

● Childcare and children at work

LOOKING FOR WORK

If you are looking for work, or you are thinking of changing your job, there are a number of ways you can find out about work opportunities. The Home Office provides guidance on who is allowed to work in the UK. Not everyone in the UK is allowed to work and some people need work permits, so it is important to check your status before taking up work. Also, employers have to check that anyone they employ is legally entitled to work in the UK. For more information and guidance, see the Home Office website 'Working in the UK' – **www.workingintheuk.gov.uk**

Jobs are usually advertised in local and national newspapers, at the local Jobcentre and in employment agencies. You can find the address and telephone number of your local Jobcentre under Jobcentre Plus in the phone book or see: **www.jobcentreplus.gov.uk**. Some jobs are advertised on supermarket notice boards and in shop windows. These jobs are usually part-time and the wages are often quite low. If there are particular companies you would like to work for, you can look for vacancies on their websites.

Jobcentre Plus is run by a government department - the Department for Work and Pensions. Trained staff give advice and help in finding and applying for jobs as well as claiming benefits. They can also arrange for interpreters. Their website, **www.jobcentreplus.gov.uk**, lists vacancies and training opportunities and gives general information on benefits. There is also a low cost telephone service – Jobseeker Direct, 0845 60 60 234. This is open 9am to 6pm on weekdays and 9am to 1pm on Saturdays.

Qualifications

Applicants for some jobs need special training or qualifications. If you have qualifications from another country, you can find out how they compare with qualifications in the UK at the National Academic Recognition Information Centre (NARIC), **www.naric.org.uk**

For further information contact UK NARIC, ECCTIS Ltd, Oriel House, Oriel Road, Cheltenham, Glos, GL50 1XP, telephone: 0870 990 4088, email: info@naric.org.uk

Applications

Interviews for lower paid and local jobs can often be arranged by telephone or in person. For many jobs you need to fill in an application form or send a copy of your curriculum vitae (CV) with a covering letter or letter of application.

A covering letter is usually a short letter attached to a completed application form, while a letter of application gives more detailed information on why you are applying for the job and why you think you are suitable. Your CV gives specific details on your education, qualifications, previous employment, skills and interests. It is important to type any letters and your CV on a computer or word processor as this improves your chance of being called for an interview.

Employers often ask for the names and addresses of one or two referees. These are people such as your current or previous employer or college tutor. Referees need to know you well and to agree to write a short report or reference on your suitability for the job. Personal friends or members of your family are not normally acceptable as referees.

Interviews

In job descriptions and interviews, employers should give full details of what the job involves, including the pay, holidays and working conditions. If you need more information about any of these, you can ask questions in the interview. In fact, asking some questions in the interview shows you are interested and can improve your chance of getting the job.

When you are applying for a job and during the interview, it is important to be honest about your qualifications and experience. If an employer later finds out that you gave incorrect information, you might lose your job.

Criminal record

For some jobs, particularly if the work involves working with children or vulnerable people, the employer will ask for your permission to do a criminal record check. You can get more information on this from the Home Office Criminal Records Bureau (CRB) information line, telephone 0870 90 90 811. In Scotland, contact Disclosure Scotland: **www.disclosurescotland.co.uk** Helpline: 0870 609 6006.

Training

Taking up training helps people improve their qualifications for work. Some training may be offered at work or you can do courses from home or at your local college. This includes English language training. You can get more information from your local library and college or from websites such as **www.worktrain.gov.uk** and **www.learndirect.co.uk**. Learndirect offers a range of online training courses at centres across the country. There are charges for courses but you can do free starter or taster sessions. You can get more information from their free information and advice line: 0800 100 900.

Volunteering and work experience

Some people do voluntary work and this can be a good way to support your local community and organisations which depend on volunteers. It also provides useful experience that can help with future job applications. Your local library will have information about volunteering opportunities.

You can also get information and advice from websites such as:

● **www.do-it.org.uk**

● **www.volunteering.org.uk**

● **www.justdosomething.net**

REVISION QUESTIONS

Check your understanding of this section by completing the questions below. Check your answers on page 198.

147	How can you check if you are allowed to work in the UK?
	ANSWER
148	Where can you get advice on how qualifications from overseas compare with qualifications from the UK?
	ANSWER
149	What is a CV?
	ANSWER
150	What is a referee?
	ANSWER
151	What might happen if any of the information you give in a job application is untrue?
	ANSWER
152	When might you need a CRB check?
	ANSWER
153	Where can you find out about training opportunities and job seeking?
	ANSWER
154	What are the benefits of volunteering?
	ANSWER

EQUAL RIGHTS AND DISCRIMINATION

It is against the law for employers to discriminate against someone at work. This means that a person should not be refused work, training or promotion or treated less favourably because of their:

- sex
- nationality, race, colour or ethnic group
- disability
- religion
- sexual orientation
- age

In Northern Ireland, the law also bans discrimination on grounds of religious belief or political opinion.

The law also says that men and women who do the same job, or work of equal value, should receive equal pay. Almost all the laws protecting people at work apply equally to people doing part-time or full-time jobs.

There are, however, a small number of jobs where discrimination laws do not apply. For example, discrimination is not against the law when the job involves working for someone in their own home.

You can get more information about the law and racial discrimination from the Commission for Racial Equality. The Equal Opportunities Commission can help with sex discrimination issues and the Disability Rights Commission deals with disability issues. Each of these organisations offers advice and information and can, in some cases, support individuals. From October 2007 their functions will be brought together in a new Commission for Equality and Human Rights. You can get more information about the laws protecting people at work from the Citizens Advice Bureau website: **www.adviceguide.org.uk**

In Northern Ireland, the Equality Commission provides information and advice in respect of all forms of unlawful discrimination.

The Commission for Racial Equality, St Dunstan's House,
201–211 Borough High Street, London, SE1 1GZ
telephone: 020 7939 000, fax: 020 7939 0001, **www.cre.gov.uk**

The Equal Opportunities Commission, Arndale House, Arndale Centre,
Manchester, M4 3EQ
telephone: 0845 601 5901, fax: 0161 838 8312, **www.eoc.org.uk**

The Disability Rights Commission, DRC Helpline,
FREEPOST MID02164, Stratford upon Avon, CV37 9BR
telephone: 08457 622 633, fax: 08457 778 878, **www.drc.org.uk**

The Equality Commission for Northern Ireland,
Equality House, 7–9 Shaftesbury Square, Belfast, BT2 7DP
telephone: 028 90 500600, **www.equalityni.org**

SEXUAL HARASSMENT

Sexual harassment can take different forms. This includes:

● indecent remarks

● comments about the way you look that make you feel uncomfortable or humiliated

● comments or questions about your sex life

● inappropriate touching or sexual demands

● bullying behaviour or being treated in a way that is rude, hostile, degrading or humiliating because of your sex

Men and women can be victims of sexual harassment at work. If this happens to you, tell a friend, colleague or trade union representative and ask the person harassing you to stop. It is a good idea to keep a written record of what happened, the days and times when it happened and who else may have seen or heard the harassment. If the problem continues, report the person to your employer or trade union. Employers are responsible for the behaviour of their employees while they are at work. They should treat complaints of sexual harassment very seriously and take effective action to deal with the problem. If you are not satisfied with your employer's response, you can ask for advice and support from the Equal Opportunities Commission, your trade union or the Citizens Advice Bureau.

REVISION QUESTIONS

Check your understanding of this section by completing the questions below.
Check your answers on page 194.

155 What does the law state about discrimination at work?

ANSWER

156 What does the law state about pay for men and women who do the same job?

ANSWER

157 List the different commissions working to promote equal opportunities and help combat discrimination

ANSWER

158 What forms could sexual harassment take and form grounds for a complaint?

ANSWER

AT WORK

Both employers and employees have legal responsibilities at work. Employers have to pay employees for the work that they do, treat them fairly and take responsible care for their health and safety. Employees should do their work with reasonable skill and care and follow all reasonable instructions. They should not damage their employer's business.

A written contract or statement

Within two months of starting a new job, your employer should give you a written contract or statement with all the details and conditions for your work. This should include your responsibilities, pay, working hours, holidays, sick pay and pension. It should also include the period of notice that both you and your employer should give for the employment to end. The contract or written statement is an important document and is very useful if there is ever a disagreement about your work, pay or conditions.

Pay, hours and holidays

Your pay is agreed between you and your employer. There is a minimum wage in the UK that is a legal right for every employed person above compulsory school leaving age. The compulsory school leaving age is 16, but the time in the school year when 16-year-olds can leave school in England and Wales is different from that in Scotland and Northern Ireland.

16-17 year olds

£3.30
an hour

18-21 year olds

£4.45
an hour

22 and above

£5.35
an hour

There are different minimum wage rates for different age groups. From October 2006 the rates are as follows:

● for workers aged 22 and above – £5.35 an hour

● for 18–21 years old – £4.45 an hour

● for 16–17 years old – £3.30 an hour.

Employers who pay their workers less than this are breaking the law. You can get more information from the Central Office of Information Directgov website, **www.direct.gov.uk** which has a wide range of public service information. Alternatively, you can telephone the National Minimum Wage Helpline, telephone: 0845 600 0678.

Your contract or statement will show the number of hours you are expected to work. Your employer might ask you if you can work more hours than this and it is your decision whether or not you do. Your employer cannot require you to work more hours than the hours agreed on your contract.

If you need to be absent from work, for example if you are ill or you have a medical appointment, it is important to tell your employer as soon as you can in advance. Most employees who are 16 or over are entitled to at least four weeks, paid holiday every year. This includes time for national holidays (see chapter 3). Your employer must give you a pay slip, or a similar written statement, each time you are paid. This must show exactly how much money has been taken off for tax and national insurance contributions.

Tax

For most people, tax is automatically taken from their earnings by the employer and paid directly to HM Revenue and Customs, the government department responsible for collecting taxes. If you are self-employed, you need to pay your own tax (see **Working for yourself**). Money raised from income tax pays for government services such as roads, education, police and the armed forces. Occasionally HM Revenue and Customs sends out tax return forms which ask for full financial details. If you receive one, it is important to complete it and return the form as soon as possible. You can get help and advice from the HM Revenue and Customs self-assessment helpline, on: 0845 300 45 55.

National Insurance

Almost everybody in the UK who is in paid work, including self-employed people, must pay National Insurance (NI) contributions. Money raised from NI contributions is used to pay contributory benefits such as the State Retirement Pension and helps fund the National Health Service. Employees have their NI contributions deducted from their pay by their employer every week or month. People who are self-employed need to pay NI contributions themselves: Class 2 contributions, either by direct debit or every three months and Class 4 contributions on the profits from their trade or business. Class 4 contributions are paid alongside their income tax. Anyone who does not pay enough NI contributions will not be able to receive certain benefits, such as Jobseeker's Allowance or Maternity Pay, and may not receive a full state retirement pension.

Getting a National Insurance number

Just before their 16th birthday, all young people in the UK are sent a National Insurance number. This is a unique number for each person and it tracks their National Insurance contributions.

Refugees whose asylum applications have been successful have the same rights to work as any other UK citizen and to receive a National Insurance number. People who have applied for asylum and have not received a positive decision do not usually have permission to work and so do not get a National Insurance number.

You need a National Insurance number when you start work. If you do not have a National Insurance number, you can apply for one through Jobcentre Plus or your local Social Security Office. It is a good idea to make an appointment by telephone and ask which documents you need to take with you. You usually need to show your birth certificate, passport and Home Office documents allowing you to stay in the country. If you need information about registering for a National Insurance number, you can telephone the National Insurance Registrations Helpline on 0845 91 57006 or 0845 91 55670.

Pensions

Everyone in the UK who has paid enough National Insurance contributions will get a State Pension when they retire. The State Pension age for men is currently 65 years of age and for women it is 60, but the State Pension age for women will increase to 65 in stages between 2010 and 2020. You can find full details of the State Pension scheme on the State Pension website, **www.thepensionservice. gov.uk** or you can phone the Pension Service Helpline: 0845 60 60 265.

In addition to a State Pension, many people also receive a pension through their work and some also pay into a personal pension plan too. It is very important to get good advice about pensions. The Pensions Advisory Service gives free and confidential advice on occupational and personal pensions. Their helpline telephone number is 0845 601 2923 and their website address is **www.opas.org. uk**. Independent financial advisers can also give advice but you usually have to pay a fee for this service. You can find local financial advisers in the Yellow Pages and Thomson local guides or on the internet at **www.unbiased.co.uk**

Health and safety

Employers have a legal duty to make sure the workplace is safe. Employees also have a legal duty to follow safety regulations and to work safely and responsibly. If you are worried about health and safety at your workplace, talk to your supervisor, manager or trade union representative. You need to follow the right procedures and your employer must not dismiss you or treat you unfairly for raising a concern.

Trade unions

Trade unions are organisations that aim to improve the pay and working conditions of their members. They also give their members advice and support on problems at work. You can choose whether to join a trade union or not and your employer cannot dismiss you or treat you unfairly for being a union member.

You can find details of trade unions in the UK, the benefits they offer to members and useful information on rights at work on the Trades Union Congress (TUC) website, **www.tuc.org.uk**

Problems at work

If you have problems of any kind at work, speak to your supervisor, manager, trade union representative or someone else with responsibility as soon as possible. If you need to take any action, it is a good idea to get advice first. If you are a member of a trade union, your representative will help. You can also contact your local Citizens Advice Bureau (CAB) or Law Centre. The national Advisory, Conciliation and Arbitration Service (ACAS) website, **www.acas.org.uk** gives information on your rights at work. ACAS also offers a national helpline, telephone: 08457 47 47 47.

Losing your job and unfair dismissal

An employee can be dismissed immediately for serious misconduct at work. Anyone who cannot do their job properly, or is unacceptably late or absent from work, should be given a warning by their employer. If their work, punctuality or attendance does not improve, the employer can give them notice to leave their job.

It is against the law for employers to dismiss someone from work unfairly. If this happens to you, or life at work is made so difficult that you feel you have to leave, you may be able to get compensation if you take your case to an Employment Tribunal. This is a court which specialises in employment matters. You normally only have three months to make a complaint.

If you are dismissed from your job, it is important to get advice on your case as soon as possible. You can ask for advice and information on your legal rights and the best action to take from your trade union representative, a solicitor, a Law Centre or the Citizens Advice Bureau.

Redundancy

If you lose your job because the company you work for no longer needs someone to do your job, or cannot afford to employ you, you may be entitled to redundancy pay. The amount of money you receive depends on the length of time you have been employed. Again your trade union representative, a solicitor, a Law Centre or the Citizens Advice Bureau can advise you.

Unemployment

Most people who become unemployed can claim Jobseeker's Allowance (JSA). This is currently available for men aged 18–65 and women aged 18-60 who are capable of working, available for work and trying to find work. Unemployed 16 and 17 year olds may not be eligible for Jobseeker's Allowance but may be able to claim a Young Person's Bridging Allowance (YPBA) instead. The local Jobcentre

Plus can help with claims. You can get further information from the Citizens Advice Bureau and the Jobcentre Plus website: **www.jobcentreplus.gov.uk**

New Deal

New Deal is a government programme that aims to give unemployed people the help and support they need to get into work. Young people who have been unemployed for 6 months and adults who have been unemployed for 18 months are usually required to join New Deal if they wish to continue receiving a benefit. There are different New Deal schemes for different age groups. You can find out more about New Deal on 0845 606 2626 or: **www.newdeal.gov.uk**

The government also runs work-based learning programmes which offer training to people while they are at work. People receive a wage or an allowance and can attend college for one day a week to get a new qualification.

You can find out more about the different government schemes, and the schemes in your area, from Jobcentre Plus, **www.jobcentreplus.gov.uk** or your local Citizens Advice Bureau.

Working for yourself

Tax

Self-employed people are responsible for paying their own tax and National Insurance. They have to keep detailed records of what they earn and spend on the business and send their business accounts to HM Revenue and Customs every year. Most self-employed people use an accountant to make sure they pay the correct tax and claim all the possible tax allowances.

As soon as you become self-employed you should register yourself for tax and National Insurance by ringing the HM Revenue and Customs telephone helpline for people who are self-employed, on 0845 915 4515.

Help and advice

Banks can give information and advice on setting up your own business and offer start-up loans, which need to be repaid with interest. Government grants and other financial support may be available. You can get details of these and advice on becoming self-employed from Business Link, a government-funded project for people starting or running a business **www.businesslink.gov.uk** telephone: 0845 600 9 006.

Working in Europe

British citizens can work in any country that is a member of the European Economic Area (EEA). In general, they have the same employment rights as a citizen of that country or state.

REVISION QUESTIONS

Check your understanding of this section by completing the questions below. Check your answers on page 199.

159 Why is it important to have a contract of employment?

ANSWER

160 What are the three minimum wage bands?

ANSWER

161 What information must be provided on pay slips?

ANSWER

162 What is the role of a trade union?

ANSWER

163 Where can you get advice if you are having problems at work?

ANSWER

164 Give two reasons why you can be dismissed from your work

ANSWER

165 What is an Employment Tribunal?

ANSWER

166 Where can you go for help if you have lost your job?

ANSWER

167 If you believe that you have unfairly lost your job, what are the timescales for complaining?

ANSWER

168 When might you be entitled to redundancy pay?

ANSWER

169 What is normally deducted from your earnings and why?

ANSWER

170 How is tax different for people who are self-employed or employed?

ANSWER

171 Where can you get help if you need it when filling out tax forms?

ANSWER

172 What happens if you do not pay enough National Insurance contributions?

ANSWER

173 How can you get a National Insurance number?

ANSWER

174 Who is entitled to a state pension?

ANSWER

175 At what age can men and women get a state pension?

ANSWER

176 What are the obligations for employers and employees regarding health and safety at work?

ANSWER

177 What should you do if you have health and safety concerns in your workplace?

ANSWER

178 What two tax responsibilities only apply to self-employed people?

ANSWER

179 What is the role of Business Link?

ANSWER

CHILDCARE AND CHILDREN AT WORK

New mothers and fathers

Women who are expecting a baby have a legal right to time off work for antenatal care. They are also entitled to at least 26 weeks maternity leave. These rights apply to full-time and part-time workers and it makes no difference how long the woman has worked for her employer. It is, however, important to follow the correct procedures and to give the employer enough notice about taking maternity leave. Some women may also be entitled to maternity pay but this depends on how long they have been working for their employer.

Fathers who have worked for their employer for at least 26 weeks are entitled to paternity leave, which provides up to two weeks time off from work, with pay, when the child is born. It is important to tell your employer well in advance.

You can get advice and more information on maternity and paternity matters from the personnel officer at work, your trade union representative, your local Citizens Advice Bureau, the Citizens Advice Bureau website **www.adviceguide.org.uk** or the government website **www.direct.gov.uk**

Childcare

It is Government policy to help people with childcare responsibilities to take up work. Some employers can help with this. The Childcarelink website **www.childcarelink.gov.uk** gives information about different types of childcare and registered childminders in your area, or telephone 08000 96 02 96.

Hours and time for children at work

In the UK there are strict laws to protect children from exploitation and to make sure that work does not get in the way of their education. The earliest legal age for children to do paid work is 13, although not all local authorities allow this. There are exceptions for some types of performance work (including modelling) when younger children may be allowed to work. Any child under school leaving age (16) seeking to do paid work must apply for a licence from the local authority. Children taking part in some kinds of performances may have to obtain a medical certificate before working.

By law, children under 16 can only do light work. There are particular jobs that children are not allowed to do. These include delivering milk, selling alcohol, cigarettes or medicines, working in a kitchen or behind the counter of a chip shop, working with dangerous machinery or chemicals, or doing any other kind of work that may be harmful to their health or education.

The law sets out clear limits for the working hours and times for 13–16 year old children. Every child must have at least two consecutive weeks a year during the school holidays when they do not work. They cannot work:

- for more than 4 hours without a one hour rest break
- for more than 2 hours on any school day or a Sunday
- more than five hours (13–14 year olds) or eight hours (15–16 year olds) on Saturdays (or weekdays during school holidays)
- before 7am or after 7pm
- before the close of school hours (except in areas where local bylaws allow children to work one hour before school)
- for more than 12 hours in any school week
- for more than 25 hours a week (13–14 year olds) or 35 hours a week (15–16 year olds) during school holidays.

There is no national minimum wage for those under 16.

The local authority may withdraw a child's licence to work, for example where a child works longer hours than the law allows. The child would then be unable to continue to work. An employer may be prosecuted for illegally employing a child. A parent or carer who makes a false declaration in a child's licence application can also be prosecuted. They may also be prosecuted if they do not ensure their child receives a proper education. You can find more information on the TUC website **www.worksmart.org.uk**

REVISION QUESTIONS

Check your understanding of this section by completing the questions below. Check your answers on page 201.

180	What must you do to ensure you receive your entitlement to maternity or paternity leave?
	ANSWER

181	What is the earliest legal age that a child can be employed for work?
	ANSWER

182	What are some of the jobs that children under 16 are not allowed to do?
	ANSWER

183	What is the maximum number of hours that a child (aged 13–16) is allowed to work in a school week?
	ANSWER

184 What must children under 16 get from their local authority before they can work?

ANSWER

185 What are the responsibilities of parents for protecting children at work?

ANSWER

EXTRA REVISION NOTES

Timeline of British History

This page lists all the key dates in British history that are mentioned in the official study materials.

1530s	Church of England established
1801	First census held in the UK
mid 1840s	Famine in Ireland
1857	Women granted right to divorce
1882	Women granted right to keep earnings and assets when married
1918	Women over 30 granted right to vote
1918	First World War ends
1922	Northern Ireland Parliament established
1928	Women granted right to vote at the same age as men
1939	Second World War begins
1945	Second World War ends
1948	National Health Service (NHS) established
1948	People from Ireland & the West Indies invited to migrate to the UK
1949	Council of Europe created
1957	Treaty of Rome signed and EEC established
1969	Voting age changed to 18
1969	Troubles break out in Northern Ireland
1972	Northern Ireland Parliament abolished
1973	Britain joins the European Union
1997	Programme to devolve power from central UK government begins
1999	Creation of the Assembly for Wales and the Scottish Parliament
2001	Last UK census held
2004	Ten new member countries join the EU
2011	Next UK census

British Calendar

This page lists all the key dates of the British calendar that are mentioned in the official study materials.

1 January	New Year
14 February	Valentine's Day
1 March	St David's Day
17 March	St Patrick's Day
three weeks before Easter	Mothering Sunday
1 April	April Fool's Day
23 April	St George's Day
31 October	Halloween
5 November	Guy Fawkes Night
11 November	Remembrance Day
30 November	St Andrew's Day
24 December	Christmas Eve
25 December	Christmas Day
26 December	Boxing Day
31 December	Hogmanay

WORDS TO KNOW

Below is a list of terms that are used within the official study materials. You will need to know the meaning of some of the terms for the Life in the UK Test. Other terms have been included as background information to help you understand some of the important concepts and facts in the study guide.

A Levels	A Levels are the examinations taken by students in their last year at school, when aged 18
A/S Levels	A/S Levels are the examinations taken by students in their second to last year at school, when aged 17
Anglican Church	The Anglican Church is also known as the Church of England
Ante-natal care	Medical care given to a woman (and to her unborn baby) while she is pregnant
April Fool's Day	April Fool's Day is the first day in April. People celebrate it by playing jokes on each other
Archbishop of Canterbury	The Archbishop of Canterbury is the head of the Anglican Church
Aristocracy	Traditionally a class of society which enjoyed inherited wealth and privilege
Asylum	A right to remain in a foreign country granted to someone who would be in danger if they returned to their home country
Bank holidays	Bank holidays are public holidays when banks and most businesses must close. They have no religious or national significance
Binge drinking	Binge drinking is drinking alcohol to excess. In recent years it has become a major focus of concerns about public disorder and minor crime
Bishop	A Bishop is a senior figure in a Christian church
Boxing Day	Boxing Day is celebrated on 26 December
British Empire	The British Empire included the countries and lands formerly colonised by Britain in Africa, the Caribbean, North America, Asia and Australasia

Building society	A financial institution, similar to a bank, which is owned by its members (rather than by shareholders) and specialises in providing mortgages and holding deposits for its members
Bureaux de change	A financial service that exchanges currencies from different countries
Bursary	Money in the form of a grant that a university gives to a student to assist them with the costs of their studies
By-election	A by-election is an election held when the representative in a particular constituency either resigns or dies
Cabinet	Cabinet is a committee of about 20 Government Ministers, chaired by the Prime Minister, who meet weekly to decide Government policy
Census	The Census is a government survey, held every 10 years, that must be completed by all residents
Chancellor of the Exchequer	The Chancellor of the Exchequer is the Minister responsible for economic policy
Chief Moderator	Head of the Presbyterian Church
Civil Service	The Civil Service are independent managers and administrators who carry out Government policy
Cockney	Cockney is the regional dialect of people who live in London
Commonwealth	The Commonwealth is an international organisation with a membership of 53 states. It arose out of the remains of the British Empire
Compensation	Money which is paid to someone to make up for suffering that they have experienced
Constituency	A constituency is a local area used in elections. People vote for an individual to represent their constituency in the House of Commons
Constitution	A constitution is a set of rules for how a country is governed
Coronation	Coronation is the ceremony held when a new Monarch is confirmed

Council of Europe	The Council of Europe is made up of most European states. It works to protect human rights and find solutions to European problems
Council of Ministers	The Council of Ministers is made up of Ministers from EU states. It proposes new laws and makes decisions about how the EU is run
Credit Union	A financial institution, owned and controlled by members, who pool their savings in order to make loans
Curriculum	A programme of education, set by the government, that must be followed by schools
Day patient	A person who spends several hours during the day in hospital for treatment
Devolved administration	Devolved administration is the principle of central government passing on its powers to regional bodies. This means decisions about certain government issues can be taken by regional parliaments, such as the Assembly for Wales
Direct debit	A payment (often a bill or membership fee) made from a bank or building society account to an organisation with the express agreement of the account holder
Divorce	Divorce is the legal ending of a marriage
D-plates	Signs attached to a car, in Wales, to indicate that the driver is learning to drive
Dual carriageway	A dual carriageway refers to any road that has physically separated lanes (by either a central barrier or strip of land, known as a central reservation or median)
Electoral Register	The electoral register is the list of all people eligible to vote in elections
European Commission	The European Commission is the civil service organisation, based in Brussels, that is responsible for running the activities of the EU
European Economic Community	A former name for the EU

European Union (EU)	An organisation of 27 member states. It allows members to cooperate, particularly on economic matters
Faith schools	Schools that are linked to a particular religion
Father Christmas	Father Christmas (also known as Santa Claus) is a mythical figure who distributes presents to children at Christmas
First Past the Post	First Past the Post is the electoral system used in the UK
Football Association (FA)	The Football Association is responsible for running the game of football in England
Foreign Secretary	The Foreign Secretary is the Minister responsible for foreign policy and Britain's relationship with other countries
Free press	Free press means that the media in Britain is not controlled by the Government
Gaelic	Gaelic is the native language of Scotland
Gap year	A break from study taken by a young person between school and university, often spent travelling and doing voluntary work
GCSE	An abbreviation for the General Certificate of Secondary Education. GCSE examinations are sat by students at the age of 16
General Election	A General Election is held at least every five years to elect members of the House of Commons
General Practitioner	A GP is a local family doctor who coordinates the health care a patient receives
Geordie	Geordie is the regional dialect of people who live in Tyneside or Newcastle upon Tyne
Grand National	The Grand National is a horse race held once a year in April
Guy Fawkes Night	Guy Fawkes Night is held annually to celebrate the thwarting of a plot to bomb the Houses of Parliament in 1605

Hansard	Hansard is one of the official records of proceedings in parliament
Hard drugs	Hard drugs are the most serious of illegal drugs, such as heroin and cocaine
Hereditary Peers	Hereditary Peers used to make up the House of Lords. They inherited their places from their parents
Home Secretary	The Home Secretary is the Minister responsible for law and order and immigration
House of Commons	The House of Commons is the lower parliamentary assembly
House of Lords	The House of Lords is the upper parliamentary assembly
Houses of Parliament	The Houses of Parliament is used to describe both the House of Commons and the House of Lords
Independent candidate	An independent candidate is a person who tries to be elected to Parliament, but is not part of a political party
Independent schools	Private schools where all educational costs are met by children's parents
In-patient	A person who needs to stay overnight for treatment in hospital
Insurance	An arrangement where a company accepts the risk of costs caused by damage to property and other possessions in exchange for regular payments, known as premiums, from the owner
Integrated schools	Schools, in Northern Ireland only, which aim to educate children from different faiths together
Islamic (Sharia) mortgages	A loan for the purchase of a home which does not require interest to be paid
Leader of the Opposition	The Leader of the Opposition is the leader of the second largest party in parliament
Legislation	Legislation is the general name given to all laws
Life Peers	Life Peers are appointed by the Prime Minister to sit in the House of Lords
Lord Chancellor	The Lord Chancellor is the government minister responsible for legal affairs

L-plates	Signs attached to a car to indicate that the driver is learning to drive
Magistrate	A person who can act as a judge in legal cases involving allegations of minor crime
Maternity leave	A period of time in which a new mother may have paid time off work to give birth and care for her new child
Member of Parliament (MP)	A Member of Parliament is a representative of the people, elected to sit in the House of Commons
Metropolitan Police	The Metropolitan Police is the police force that serves the people of London
Minister	A Minister is a senior Government politician with policy and other responsibilities
Monarch	The head of state. Used to describe the Queen or King
Mortgage	A loan for the purchase of a home
MOT	A yearly compulsory (Ministry of Transport) test that a vehicle is safe to be driven
Mothering Sunday	Mothering Sunday is a day of celebration where children show appreciation to their mothers
National Assembly for Wales	The National Assembly for Wales is where Welsh representatives meet to determine matters of policy. It is located in Cardiff
National Insurance	A form of compulsory tax that is used to fund health and welfare services and the state pension
New Scotland Yard	New Scotland Yard is the headquarters of the Metropolitan Police
Non-departmental Public Bodies	Non-departmental public bodies are agencies set up and funded by the government. They have greater independence than government departments and are generally allowed to operate without any direct control by the ministers or departments that create them. They are also sometimes known as quangos
Off-licence	A shop that sells alcoholic drinks for consumption off the premises (as opposed to a bar or pub)
Outpatient	A person who attends a hospital for treatment for a brief time during the day

Palace of Westminster	The Palace of Westminster houses the House of Commons and the House of Lords
Parliament	Parliament is where elected national representatives meet to discuss issues and develop laws
Parliament of Scotland	The Parliament of Scotland, situated in Edinburgh, represents the Scottish people
Parliamentary democracy	A parliamentary democracy describes a country where decisions of government are made by a parliament of representatives
Party system	A party system is a political system in which representatives and voters organise themselves into groups. These groups usually have shared values and goals.
Paternity leave	A period of time when the father of a newly born child may take paid time off work to care for the child
Patron Saint	A Christian saint that is traditionally thought to protect a country and its people
PIN	Personal Identification Number. A code that a person keeps secret that enables them to access money and make purchases using a debit, credit or store card
Presbyterian Church	The Presbyterian Church is the Church of Scotland
Pressure Groups	Pressure groups are group with special interests who seek to influence politicians
Prime Minister	The Prime Minister is the leader of the governing party and chair of the Cabinet
Proportional Representation	Proportional Representation is an electoral system where seats in parliament are allocated to parties according to the proportion of votes received
Protestant	A Protestant is a person that belongs to a particular Christian religion. This includes members of the Anglican Church and the Presbyterian Church
Quango	Quango is another name for a non-departmental public body

Queen's Speech	The Queen's Speech is delivered by the Queen at the beginning of a new session of parliament setting out Government policies and intentions
Redundancy	The loss of a job when the employer no longer needs an employee to perform the particular role or can no longer afford to pay for the role
Reformation	The Reformation was a movement in the sixteenth century that installed Protestantism as the established religion in Britain
Remembrance Day	Remembrance Day is held each November to remember those who have died at war
Road tax	A tax that must be paid on a vehicle before it can be driven on public roads
R-plates	Signs attached to a car, in Northern Ireland, to indicate that the driver is learning to drive
Scouse	Scouse is the regional dialect of people who live in Liverpool
Shadow Cabinet	The Shadow Cabinet is a group of MPs from the main opposition party in Parliament who are responsible for representing the party on important issues
Single carriageway	A single carriageway refers to any road that does not have any physical separation between lanes of opposing flows of traffic. A one-way street is also a single carriageway
Solicitor	A qualified lawyer who gives legal advice and has an important role in the buying and selling of property
Speaker	The Speaker in both the House of Commons and House of Lords acts as chair in parliamentary debates
Standing order	A standing order is an instruction a bank account holder gives to their bank to pay a set amount at regular intervals to another account
State pension	A regular payment of money by the government to a citizen who has reached retirement age
Stepfamily	A stepfamily is formed when people with children re-marry

Stormont	Stormont is the name of the building where the Northern Ireland Assembly meets
Supreme Governor	The Supreme Governor is the role performed by the Monarch as head of the Anglican Church
Surveyor	A person who provides a check on the condition of a house before it is sold
Tenancy	The period of time that a landlord and tenant agree that a home shall be rented
Tenancy agreement	A legal document that records the agreement reached between a landlord and a tenant to rent a home
Trade union	A group of workers with common interests. It advocates for its members and protects their legal employment rights
United Nations (UN)	The United Nations is a global organisation dedicated to peace, security and human rights
United Nations Security Council	The United Nations Security Council is a committee of 15 members focused on global security. The UK is one of five permanent members
Voluntary work	Work that is done without pay, often for a charity
Vulnerable people	People who are disadvantaged in society and may not be able to protect their own interests
Whips	Whips are MPs who ensure other MPs from their political party cast their vote in line with party intentions
Wimbledon	Wimbledon is a prestigious tennis tournament held annually in south London

PRACTICE TESTS

Preparation Tips

Before you start

The Life in the UK Test is made up of 24 multiple choice questions. You have 45 minutes to complete the test. This means you have just under two minutes to answer each question. This is plenty of time as long as you concentrate and work steadily. However, don't spend too much time on one question. If you find a question difficult and are unsure of the correct answer then make a note of the question number on your blank paper. Come back to the question once you have completed the rest of the test.

Before you begin the test ask the test supervisor for blank paper. You will not be able to use any other materials during the test however you can use the supplied paper to make notes during the test, particularly about any questions you find difficult and want to come back to later.

Questions to expect

ALL questions in the *Life in the UK Test* are multiple choice format. There are four different formats in which a question may be asked:

1. One correct answer – Choose the correct answer to the question from four options

EXAMPLE

When did women first get the right to vote?

A   1840

B   1901

C   1918

D   1945

2. Two correct answers – Choose two correct answers to the question from four options

EXAMPLE

The UK restricted its immigration laws in the 1970s - however which TWO locations did Britain admit refugees from during this time?

A   Ethiopia

B   South East Asia

C   Turkey

D   Uganda

3. True or False – Decide whether a statement is true or false

EXAMPLE

Judges are independent of the Crown. Is this statement true or false?

A   True

B   False

4. Select correct statement – Choose the correct statement from two options

EXAMPLE

Which of these statements is correct?

A   The House of Lords may reject laws proposed by the House of Commons

B   The House of Lords can only delay the passage of new laws

Working through the answers

When you start your test make sure you read each question carefully. Make sure you understand it.

If you are confident that you know the correct answer then make your selection and move on to the next question.

It is vital that you select an answer for every question even if you are not confident that it is correct. There is a chance that even a guess will be correct! If you do this make sure that you note the question number on your blank paper. It is possible that a question later in the test will help you to answer a question that you have found difficult.

Traps to watch out for

 Some questions may be worded so that an option may be a TRUE statement but not be the CORRECT answer to the question being asked.

Be careful if questions and answers use words that are *absolute*. These words mean that the question or answer applies in all cases (e.g. *always, every*) or not at all (e.g. *never*).

EXAMPLE

Which of these statements is correct?

A   *The Queen must always marry someone who is Protestant*

B   *The Queen must always marry someone who is British*

This question gives the option between two very absolute statements. There are no exceptions. In this example, the correct answer is A. The Monarch swears to maintain the Protestant religion in Britain, and must always marry another Protestant.

You also need to be careful of words that *moderate* a question or answer. When words such as *often, rarely, sometimes* and *usually* are used this means that the question or answer is referring to something which is not true in all cases.

EXAMPLE

Where are government statements usually reported as coming from?

A   *Buckingham Palace*

B   *Number Ten*

C   *Stormont*

D   *Clarence House*

In the above example, it is possible that a government statement might come from other ministers or departments, however in most cases media will report most statements as coming from Number Ten. Therefore, option B is the correct answer.

Also watch for negative words in questions or answers – such as *not, never* and *neither*. These words can be easily overlooked and completely change the meaning of the question being asked.

EXAMPLE

Which of the following statements about the Commonwealth is not correct?

A   *It has a common language*

B   *It has a membership of 53 states*

C   *It has 10% of the world's population*

D   *The Crown is the symbolic head*

In the example above, notice that the question is asking for the statement that is not correct. The Commonwealth does have a common language, comprises 53 member states, and the Crown is the symbolic head. The Commonwealth is 30% of the world's population therefore, although option C is a false statement, it is the correct answer for this question.

For some questions one of the answers may read: *all of the above*. In these cases read the other answers carefully to see if it is possible that they are all correct. Even if two of the three answers seem correct, all three alternative answers must be correct for you to choose the *all of the above* option.

For some questions one of the answers may read: *none of the above*. In these cases read the other answers carefully to see if it is possible that they are all incorrect. Even if two of the three answers seem incorrect, all three alternative answers must be wrong for you to choose the *none of the above* option.

PRACTICE TEST 1

1   Why did the UK encourage immigration in the 1950s?

   A   Because of an agreement with other Commonwealth countries

   B   To meet an EU directive on immigration

   C   To offer safety to people escaping persecution

   D   To resolve a shortage of labour in the UK

2   What percentage of the workforce are women?

   A   40%

   B   45%

   C   51%

   D   65%

3   In England, when do most young people take GCSE examinations?

   A   15 years old

   B   16 years old

   C   17 years old

   D   18 years old

4   What proportion of young people who became first-time voters in the 2001 general election actually used their vote?

   A   One in two

   B   One in three

   C   One in five

   D   One in six

5   Where is the Cockney dialect spoken?

   A   Cornwall

   B   Liverpool

   C   London

   D   Tyneside

6   What percentage of Christians in the UK are Roman Catholic?

    A 10%

    B 20%

    C 30%

    D 40%

7   When is New Year celebrated in the United Kingdom?

    A 1 January

    B 1 March

    C 25 December

    D 31 December

8   When is Remembrance Day?

    A 1 May

    B 11 November

    C 21 October

    D 31 August

9   What must a candidate achieve in order to win their constituency?

    A Be a member of the party that wins government office

    B Win at least 15,000 votes

    C Win at least 25% of the votes within their constituency

    D Win the most votes out of all candidates in their constituency

10 What is the role of the Cabinet?

    A To examine laws proposed by the House of Commons

    B To investigate serious complaints against the police

    C To make decisions about government policy

    D To provide royal assent for new laws

11 Which country does not have its own parliament or national assembly?

A England

B Northern Ireland

C Scotland

D Wales

12 When are local government elections held?

A April every two years

B June and December each year

C May each year

D September each year

13 Newspaper owners and editors do not try to influence public opinion. Is this statement true or false?

A True

B False

14 How many countries are members of the European Union?

A 12 countries

B 15 countries

C 27 countries

D 41 countries

15 Where can you get a mortgage from? Select two correct answers from below

A A bank

B A building society

C An estate agent

D A housing association

16 **What is the purpose of Housing Benefit?**

    A To help you buy a home

    B To help you fix a home

    C To help you pay your rent

    D To help you sell a home

17 **Where can you get further information about welfare benefits? Select two correct answers from below**

    A A bank

    B A building society

    C Jobcentre Plus

    D Citizens Advice Bureau

18 **At what age can children in the UK choose to leave school?**

    A 12

    B 14

    C 16

    D 18

19 **People under 18 cannot drink alcohol in a pub but they can buy it in a supermarket or an off-licence. Is this statement true or false?**

    A True

    B False

20 **What is the speed limit for cars and motorcycles on motorways and dual carriageways?**

    A 100 miles per hour

    B 50 miles per hour

    C 60 miles per hour

    D 70 miles per hour

21 **Select the correct statement**

    A It is illegal to discriminate against someone for employment in any circumstances

    B It is legal to discriminate against someone if the job involves working in the employer's home

22 **Which of these statements is correct?**

    A The HM Revenue and Customs self-assessment helpline can provide help and advice on filling out tax forms

    B You can only get help filling out tax forms by paying for the services of an accountant

23 **Your employer can dismiss you for being a union member. Is this statement true or false?**

    A True

    B False

24 **Select the correct statement**

    A Only women that have full-time employment are entitled to maternity leave

    B Maternity leave rights apply to both full-time and part-time workers

PRACTICE TEST 2

1   Why were recruitment centres set up in the West Indies in the 1950s?

   A   To recruit workers for textile factories

   B   To recruit workers to build canals

   C   To recruit workers to build railways

   D   To recruit workers to drive buses

2   On average, boys leave school with better qualifications than girls. Is this statement true or false?

   A   True

   B   False

3   In Scotland, when do most young people take SQA examinations?

   A   15 years old

   B   16 years old

   C   17 years old

   D   18 years old

4   What is a census?

   A   A count of the whole population

   B   A form required for postal voting

   C   A traditional English festival

   D   The government department that collects statistics

5   Where is the Geordie dialect spoken?

   A   Cornwall

   B   Liverpool

   C   London

   D   Tyneside

6   When is the national day for Northern Ireland?

A   1 March

B   17 March

C   23 April

D   30 November

7   When is Valentine's Day?

A   1 April

B   1 February

C   14 April

D   14 February

8   What does Remembrance Day commemorate?

A   The appreciation of single mothers

B   The celebration of community

C   The crucifixion of Jesus Christ

D   The memory of those who died fighting in wars

9   What is the name of the system that governs how MPs are elected into the House of Commons?

A   Aggregated vote system

B   Electoral college system

C   First past the post system

D   Proportional representation system

10   How often does the Cabinet normally meet?

A   Bi-weekly

B   Daily

C   Monthly

D   Weekly

11 **Which policy areas have not been transferred to the Welsh Assembly or the Scottish Parliament and remain under central UK government control? Select two options from below**

  A Defence

  B Foreign affairs

  C Education

  D Health

12 **Can a judge change an Act of Parliament if it is incompatible with the Human Rights Act?**

  A Yes, but they must seek the Prime Minister's approval first

  B Yes, but they must obtain permission from the Lord Chancellor

  C Yes, but only if they believe the law is unfair

  D No, but they can ask Parliament to consider doing so

13 **Which of the following statements is correct about political reporting during election periods in the UK? Select two options from below**

  A Television channels have to give equal time to rival viewpoints

  B All reporting on radio and television must be balanced

  C It is illegal for newspapers to run campaigns to influence people's opinions

  D Politicians must be able to read interview questions beforehand

14 **When did the UK join the European Union?**

  A 1935

  B 1959

  C 1973

  D The UK is not a member of the European Union

15 **If you are buying a home in Scotland who should you approach first?**

  A A bank

  B A solicitor

  C An estate agent

  D Your local MP

16 Where should you go for help if you are homeless?

A To the local authority

B To the local hospital

C To your GP

D To your MP

17 Which of the following statements is correct?

A If you need to see a specialist for medical treatment then you must see your GP first

B You should always go directly to a specialist if you believe you know the medical treatment you require

18 Which of these statements is correct?

A Schools can choose to provide religious education to pupils

B Parents are allowed to withdraw their children from religious education lessons

19 What is the minimum age for purchasing alcohol?

A 14 years old

B 16 years old

C 17 years old

D 18 years old

20 What is the speed limit for cars and motorcycles on single carriageways?

A 60 miles per hour

B 70 miles per hour

C 80 miles per hour

D 90 miles per hour

21 What types of discrimination can the Equal Opportunities Commission help with?

A Discrimination related to disability

B Racial discrimination

C Religious discrimination

D Sex discrimination

22 What happens if you do not pay enough NI contributions? Select two options from below

A You will not be entitled to certain benefits such as Jobseeker's Allowance or Maternity Pay

B You may not receive a full state retirement pension

C You will be fined and need to sign up to a repayment plan

D You will be prosecuted and may face a prison sentence

23 It is compulsory for employees to join a trade union. Is this statement true or false?

A True

B False

24 Select the correct statement

A Men are always entitled to paternity leave

B Men must have worked for their employer at least 26 weeks before they are entitled to paternity leave

PRACTICE TEST 3

1 **Why was there a fall in the number of people migrating to the UK from the West Indies, India, Pakistan and Bangladesh in the late 1960s and early 1970s?**

    A A weak British currency made immigration less appealing

    B It was becoming more difficult for immigrants to find employment in the UK

    C New laws were introduced restricting immigration to Britain

    D These countries were experiencing labour shortages

2 **What is the difference in the average hourly pay rate for men and women?**

    A The average hourly pay rate is 5% lower for women

    B The average hourly pay rate is 10% lower for women

    C The average hourly pay rate is 20% lower for women

    D No difference – the average hourly pay rate for women is the same as men

3 **In Scotland, when do most young people take Higher/Advanced Higher Grades?**

    A 10 and 11 years old

    B 13 and 14 years old

    C 15 and 16 years old

    D 17 and 18 years old

4 **What was the population of the United Kingdom in 2005?**

    A 39.3 million

    B 49.8 million

    C 59.8 million

    D 98.3 million

5 What other regional language, in addition to English, is also spoken in Scotland?

    A French

    B Gaelic

    C Scottish

    D Welsh

6 When is the national day for England?

    A 1 March

    B 17 March

    C 23 April

    D 30 November

7 What do people sometimes do on Valentine's Day?

    A Fast from eating for the whole day

    B Play jokes on each other until midday

    C Send anonymous cards to someone they secretly admire

    D Wear poppies in memory of St Valentine

8 What do people wear on Remembrance Day in memory of those who have died at war?

    A Black clothing

    B Military clothing

    C Poppies

    D Red ribbons

9 How is it decided which party forms the Government?

    A The members of the House of Lords vote for their preferred party

    B The party that wins the majority of constituencies forms the Government

    C The party with the most candidates forms the Government

    D The party with the most votes forms the Government

10 How many politicians are there in the Cabinet?

    A About 10

    B About 20

    C About 30

    D About 40

11 Which voting system is used to elect the Scottish Parliament and the Welsh Assembly?

    A A ranking or preferential system

    B Assembly members are chosen by the government

    C 'First past the post'

    D Proportional representation

12 A judge can decide whether a person is guilty or innocent of a serious crime. Is this statement true or false?

    A True

    B False

13 Which of these statements is correct?

    A Only UK born citizens have the right to vote and duties such as jury service

    B Both UK born and naturalised citizens have the right to vote and duties such as jury service

14 Britain was a founding member of the EU. Is this statement true or false?

    A True

    B False

15 Estate agents represent the person buying a house or flat. Is this statement true or false?

    A True

    B False

16 **Which phone numbers should be called in an emergency for police, fire and ambulance services? Select two options from below**

    A 999

    B 112

    C 111

    D 911

17 **Which of these statements is correct?**

    A In an emergency you can attend a hospital, but only if you have a letter from your GP

    B In an emergency you should go to the Accident and Emergency department of your nearest hospital

18 **At what ages are Key Stage Tests held in England?**

    A 10, 12 and 14

    B 11, 15 and 17

    C 7 and 15

    D 7, 11 and 14

19 **What is the standard closing time of a pub?**

    A 10pm

    B 11pm

    C 1am

    D 2am

20 **You can not be arrested if you refuse to take a breathalyser test. Is this statement true or false?**

    A True

    B False

21 If you have a problem with your neighbours, who can you go to in order to solve the problem without taking the case to court?

A Lawyer

B Mediator

C Justice of the Peace

D Magistrate

22 What are National Insurance contributions used for? Select two options from below

A To contribute to your State Retirement Pension

B To help fund the National Health Service

C To pay for education and community services

D To pay for police and armed services

23 For what reason could you be immediately dismissed from your job?

A Because of serious misconduct

B Because of your age

C Because of your religious beliefs

D Because of your sexuality

24 How many weeks of paid paternity leave are men entitled to?

A Four weeks

B One week

C Three weeks

D Two weeks

PRACTICE TEST 4

---

1   Which of these statements is correct?

   A   In 19th century Britain, women had fewer rights than men

   B   Women have always had the same rights as men

---

2   How many young people (up to the age of 19) are there in the UK?

   A   10 million

   B   15 million

   C   20 million

   D   5 million

---

3   What is the minimum age for buying tobacco?

   A   14 years old

   B   16 years old

   C   18 years old

   D   21 years old

---

4   What is the population of England?

   A   23.4 million

   B   38.1 million

   C   50.1 million

   D   58.8 million

---

5   Where is the Welsh language widely spoken?

   A   Highlands and Islands of Scotland

   B   Ireland

   C   Southern England

   D   Wales

---

6   What is the name of the patron saint of Northern Ireland?

A   St Andrew

B   St David

C   St George

D   St Patrick

7   What traditionally happens on April Fool's Day?

A   It is a public holiday until noon

B   People enjoy public fireworks displays

C   People play jokes on each other

D   None of the above

8   What sport is played at the Wimbledon tournament?

A   Cricket

B   Football

C   Rugby

D   Tennis

9   How are Whips appointed?

A   By the King or Queen

B   By the Prime Minister

C   By their party leaders

D   By vote amongst their peers

10   What is the name of the ministerial position that is responsible for legal affairs?

A   Chancellor of the Exchequer

B   Foreign Secretary

C   Home Secretary

D   Lord Chancellor

11 **Which of the following parliaments or assemblies use proportional representation?**

    A Scottish Parliament

    B Northern Ireland Assembly

    C European Parliament

    D All of the above

12 **When can a magistrate decide whether a person is guilty or innocent?**

    A A magistrate can always decide whether a person is guilty or innocent regardless of the alleged crime

    B A magistrate can not decide whether a person is guilty or innocent; instead a jury must always be used

    C If a person is accused of having committed a minor crime

    D If a person is accused of having committed a serious crime

13 **What is the current voting age?**

    A 16 years old

    B 18 years old

    C 20 years old

    D 21 years old

14 **Which of these statements is correct?**

    A Subject to some restrictions, citizens of the European Union have the right to work in any EU member state

    B Citizens of the European Union must always have a valid work permit to work in any EU member state

15 **Who carries out checks on a house that you want to buy?**

    A A housing association

    B A landlord

    C A surveyor

    D The seller

16 How are local government services paid for? Select two options from below

A Grants from central government

B Council tax

C Charitable donations

D Insurance premiums

17 When should you look for a GP?

A As soon as you move to a new area

B Once you have registered with the local authority

C When you become ill

D When you visit the local hospital

18 What are courses for people who want to improve their English language skills called?

A EAL

B EEE

C ESOL

D NHS

19 Which of these statements is correct?

A Tickets for trains are usually bought before you get on the train

B Tickets for trains are usually bought when you have reached your destination

20 Select the correct statement

A Employers have to check that everyone they employ is legally entitled to work in the UK

B Employers can employ anyone as long as they have a UK bank account

21 **What does the government programme New Deal provide?**

A Help and support for unemployed people to get back into work

B Accommodation and support for the homeless

C Healthcare and medicines for the sick and elderly

D Funding and an advice service for small businesses

22 **At what age do young people receive their National Insurance number?**

A 14 years old

B 16 years old

C 18 years old

D 20 years old

23 **When might you be entitled to redundancy pay?**
    Select two options from below

A The job is no longer needed by the employer

B The employer can not afford to pay for the job

C If you are dismissed from your job

D If you meet performance targets set by your employer

24 **Select the correct statement**

A It is illegal to employ children under the age of 16

B You may legally employ children under the age of 16
   provided they have a licence from the local authority

PRACTICE TEST 5

1   When did married women gain the right to retain ownership of their own money and property?

    A   1752

    B   1792

    C   1810

    D   1882

2   How often do most children in the UK receive their pocket money?

    A   Every day

    B   Every month

    C   Every week

    D   Only on their birthday

3   More young people are smoking and, in particular, more girls smoke than boys. Is this statement true or false?

    A   True

    B   False

4   What is the population of Northern Ireland?

    A   0.9 million

    B   1.7 million

    C   2.5 million

    D   3.1 million

5   One of the dialects spoken in Northern Ireland is called Ulster Scots. Is this statement true or false?

    A   True

    B   False

6 **When is the national day for Scotland?**

    A 1 March

    B 17 March

    C 23 April

    D 30 November

7 **When is April Fool's Day?**

    A 1 April

    B 1 February

    C 1 March

    D 1 May

8 **What type of constitution does the UK have?**

    A A legal constitution

    B A written constitution

    C An amended constitution

    D An unwritten constitution

9 **What are the roles of the Whips in Parliament?**
Select two correct roles from below

    A Responsible for discipline in their party

    B Ensure attendance of MPs at voting time in the House of Commons

    C Ensure the House of Commons is always safe and secure

    D Keep order in the House of Commons during political debates

10 **What is the name of the ministerial position that is responsible for law, order and immigration?**

    A Chancellor of the Exchequer

    B Chief Whip

    C Home Secretary

    D Lord Chancellor

11 Which one of the following parliaments or assemblies does not use proportional representation?

A House of Commons

B Northern Ireland Assembly

C Welsh Assembly

D Scottish Parliament

12 When is a jury used?

A To choose an appropriate penalty for someone found guilty of a serious crime

B To confirm decisions made by a judge

C To decide if someone is innocent or guilty of a serious crime

D To decide if someone is innocent or guilty of a less important crime

13 It is not possible to see the electoral register as this would damage the privacy of voters. Is this statement true or false?

A True

B False

14 What is the main aim behind the European Union today?

A For member states to function as a single market

B For member states to improve efficiency

C For member states to observe a single set of laws

D For member states to protect human rights in Europe

15 Which of the following statements is correct?

A Everyone is entitled to apply for council accommodation

B Only people on benefits are entitled to apply for council accommodation

16 If you are the tenant of a property then you do not have to pay Council Tax. Is this statement true or false?

A True

B False

17 **Which of these statements is correct?**

    A Some dentists have two sets of charges, both NHS and private

    B All dentists work for the NHS

18 **University students in England, Wales and Northern Ireland do not have to pay tuition fees. Is this statement true or false?**

    A True

    B False

19 **What are two stages that you must complete before you can get a full driving licence? Choose two correct answers from below**

    A Pass a practical driving test

    B Pass an MOT test

    C Pass a written theory test

    D Pass a breathalyser test

20 **Everyone in the UK is allowed to work. Is this statement true or false?**

    A True

    B False

21 **What is the minimum wage for workers aged 22 and above?**

    A £3.30 an hour

    B £4.45 an hour

    C £5.35 an hour

    D £6.15 an hour

22 **What is the purpose of a National Insurance number?**

    A To allow companies to check your credit history

    B To prove that you have British nationality

    C To prove that you have adequate home insurance

    D To track National Insurance contributions

23   Between what ages can women claim the Jobseeker's Allowance?

A   16–65 years old

B   18–60 years old

C   18–65 years old

D   21–65 years old

24   What is the youngest legal age for children to do paid work?

A   10 years old

B   12 years old

C   13 years old

D   8 years old

PRACTICE TEST 6

1   **What year did women in the UK gain the right to divorce their husband?**

   A   1810

   B   1857

   C   1901

   D   1945

2   **What percentage of children in the UK live with both birth parents?**

   A   25%

   B   40%

   C   65%

   D   80%

3   **Which of the following statements is correct?**

   A   Electoral registration forms are available only in English

   B   Electoral registration forms are available in English, Welsh and other languages

4   **What percentage of the UK's population live in England?**

   A   53%

   B   68%

   C   75%

   D   84%

5   **According to the 2001 Census, what percentage of the UK population reported that they had a religion?**

   A   35%

   B   55%

   C   65%

   D   75%

6 When is the national day for Wales?

A 1 March

B 17 March

C 23 April

D 30 November

7 What traditionally happens on Mother's Day?

A Mothers make special meals for their families

B People celebrate the mother of Jesus Christ

C People give cards or gifts to their mothers

D People hold fireworks displays

8 The monarch rules the UK and can reject laws and decisions made by government and the Cabinet. Is this statement true or false?

A True

B False

9 What is a Life Peer?

A A hereditary aristocrat or peer of the realm

B A member of the House of Lords who has been appointed by the Prime Minister

C Any person who has inherited a peerage from their family

D Any person who has served as an MP for more than twenty years

10 What is the second largest party in the House of Commons called?

A Shadow Cabinet

B The Conservation Party

C The Labour Party

D The Opposition

11 **On which matters can the Scottish Parliament make decisions? Select two options from below**

   A Education

   B Foreign Policy

   C Defence

   D Health

12 **Who is responsible for investigating serious complaints against the police?**

   A The Home Secretary

   B The Independent Police Complaints Commission

   C The Lord Chancellor

   D The Police Commissioner

13 **What may prevent you from being able to stand for public office? Select two options from below**

   A Being a member of the armed forces

   B Having been found guilty of a criminal offence

   C Being a Commonwealth citizen

   D Being a citizen of the Irish Republic

14 **Everyone in the UK has the legal right to practise the religion of their choice. Is this statement true or false?**

   A True

   B False

15 **Which statement is correct?**

   A When you rent a home privately you sign a tenancy agreement or lease

   B When you agree to buy a home you sign a tenancy agreement or lease

16 Who should you speak to if you have trouble with your neighbours? Select two options from below

A Your landlord

B The local authority

C The bank

D Your GP

17 Which of these statements is correct?

A You can get regular ante-natal care from your local hospital, local health centre or from special ante-natal clinics

B Ante-natal care is only available from special private clinics and is not part of the NHS

18 What does the film classification PG mean?

A Children under 15 are not allowed to see or rent the film

B No one under 18 is allowed to see or rent the film

C Suitable for anyone aged four years or over

D Suitable for everyone but some parts of the film might be unsuitable for children

19 If you have a driving licence from an EU country, then you can only use it in the UK for up to 12 months. Is this statement true or false?

A True

B False

20 How can you compare qualifications from another country with those in the UK?

A By asking your neighbour

B By contacting the National Academic Recognition Information Centre

C By visiting your local library

D By writing to potential employers

21 Select the correct statement

    A It is illegal to pay workers below the minimum wage

    B It is legal to pay workers below the minimum wage as long as they agree to the wage rate

22 Where can you apply for a National Insurance number? Select two options from below

    A Any Jobcentre Plus branch

    B Your local Social Security Office

    C Your local library

    D Your local council or town hall

23 Between what ages can men claim the Jobseeker's Allowance?

    A 16–65 years old

    B 18–60 years old

    C 18–65 years old

    D 21–65 years old

24 What must children under 16 seeking to do paid work obtain before they can be employed?

    A A letter of permission from their parents or carer

    B Proof of identity

    C A licence from the local authority

    D A National Insurance number

PRACTICE TEST 7

1   Who were Suffragettes?

A   Nurses that cared for the elderly

B   Representatives of people seeking asylum

C   Refugee care workers

D   Campaigners for greater rights for women

2   What percentage of children live within a stepfamily?

A   10%

B   25%

C   40%

D   55%

3   What is a 'gap year'?

A   A measurement used by the government to assess literacy

B   A period of time taken by a young person to work or travel before starting university

C   A year of study that has to be repeated

D   The first year a young person spends at university

4   How often is a census carried out in the United Kingdom?

A   Once every eight years

B   Once every five years

C   Once every ten years

D   Whenever the government decides

5   According to the 2001 Census, what proportion of the UK population are Christians?

A   Five people out of ten

B   Nine people out of ten

C   Seven people out of ten

D   Two people out of ten

6   What is the name of the patron saint of Wales?

    A St Andrew

    B St David

    C St George

    D St Patrick

7   When is Mother's Day?

    A The Saturday four weeks before Easter

    B The Sunday four weeks before Easter

    C The Sunday one week before Easter

    D The Sunday three weeks before Easter

8   Who is the Head of State of the United Kingdom?

    A The Home Secretary

    B The King or Queen

    C The Prime Minister

    D The Speaker of the House of Commons

9   Hereditary peers have lost the automatic right to attend the House of Lords. Is this statement true or false?

    A True

    B False

10   Which politicians are members of the Shadow Cabinet?

    A Civil servants working for the government

    B Peers from the House of Lords

    C Senior members of the main opposition party

    D The remaining MPs in Government who are not in the Cabinet

11 On which matters can the Northern Ireland Assembly make decisions? Select two options from below

A Education

B Foreign Policy

C Defence

D Environment

12 The Government has the power to instruct the police to follow its instructions on what to do in a particular case. Is this statement true or false?

A True

B False

13 To become a local councillor, a candidate must have a local connection with the area. Is this statement true or false?

A True

B False

14 What is a role of the European Parliament?

A Elect individual members of the European Commission

B Ensure EU regulations and directives are being followed by member states

C Examine decisions made by the European Council and the European Commission

D Review European court cases that have been appealed

15 What is contained in an inventory, when one is attached to a tenancy agreement?

A A list of all furniture and fittings in a property

B A list of all people who have lived in a property

C A record of the rent paid for a property

D Information about the owner of a property

16 What denomination of bank notes do not exist in the UK?

    A £5

    B £20

    C £50

    D £500

17 Who provides regular contact and advice to parents after a child is born and up until it is five years old?

    A A health visitor

    B A midwife

    C A specialist

    D An optician

18 What does the film classification U means?

    A Children under 15 are not allowed to see or rent the film

    B No one under 18 is allowed to see or rent the film

    C Suitable for anyone aged four years or over

    D Suitable for everyone but some parts of the film might be unsuitable for Children

19 If you have a driving licence from a country outside the EU, you may use it in the UK for up to 12 months. Is this statement true or false?

    A True

    B False

20 Who should you ask to be a referee for a job application? Select two options from below

    A A previous employer

    B A close personal friend

    C A relative or family member

    D A college tutor

21 **It is legal for your employer to force you to work more hours than has been agreed in your contract. Is this statement true or false?**

A True

B False

22 **At what age can women get a state pension?**

A 55 years old

B 60 years old

C 65 years old

D 70 years old

23 **Which of the following statements is correct?**

A As soon as you become self-employed you should register yourself for National Insurance and tax by contacting HM Revenue and Customs

B It is not necessary to contact the HM Revenue and Customs when you become self-employed

24 **Select the correct statement from below**

A Children under 16 can be employed to do any form of work as long as they are properly trained

B It is illegal to employ children under 16 to do work that might harm their health or education

PRACTICE TEST 8

1   When were women over 30 given the right to vote?

A   1840

B   1901

C   1918

D   1945

2   What percentage of children live in lone-parent families?

A   10%

B   25%

C   40%

D   55%

3   What are the most common jobs that children in Britain do? Select two answers from below

A   Work in hospitals or pharmacies

B   Work in kitchens

C   Work in supermarkets or newsagents

D   Deliver newspapers

4   What is the largest ethnic minority in Britain?

A   Bangladeshi descent

B   Black Caribbean descent

C   Indian descent

D   Pakistani descent

5   What is the title of the King or Queen within the Church of England?

A   Archbishop of Canterbury

B   Governor General

C   Head Priest

D   Supreme Governor

6   What does Christmas Day celebrate?

   A The birth of Jesus Christ

   B The death of Jesus Christ

   C The miracles of Jesus Christ

   D The resurrection of Jesus Christ

7   When is Halloween celebrated?

   A 1 March

   B 31 October

   C 1 November

   D 30 November

8   When are general elections held?

   A At least every year

   B At least every four years

   C At least every five years

   D At least every ten years

9   What are the functions of the House of Lords?
Select two options from below

   A Suggest amendments to laws

   B Propose new laws

   C Elect the Prime Minister

   D Elect the Speaker of the House of Commons

10   What are functions of the Speaker of the House of Commons?
Select two options from below

   A To keep order during political debates

   B To make sure rules are followed in the House of Commons

   C To promote Members from the House of Commons to the House of Lords

   D To give royal assent to new laws agreed in the House of Commons

11 **The UK government cannot suspend the Northern Ireland Assembly. Is this statement true or false?**

A True

B False

12 **What is a quango?**

A A local police officer

B A non-departmental public body

C Another name for the Lord Chancellor

D The name of the British citizenship ceremony

13 **What must a candidate have in order to become a local councillor?**

A A connection with the area in which they wish to take office

B A deposit of £500

C A recommendation from their local MP

D Membership of a political party

14 **European Union law is legally binding in the UK. Is this statement true or false?**

A True

B False

15 **A deposit paid to the landlord at the beginning of a tenancy is usually equal to one month's rent. Is this statement true or false?**

A True

B False

16 **Bank notes from Scotland and Northern Ireland are not valid in the rest of the UK. Is this statement true or false?**

A True

B False

17 **What does the Family Planning Association provide advice on?**
Select two options from below

   A   Sexual heath

   B   Contraception

   C   Family values

   D   Ambulance services

18 **Which of these statements is correct?**

   A   No one younger than 18 may see an '18'
       rated film under any circumstances

   B   No one younger than 18 may see an '18' rated
       film unless they are with an adult

19 **Which of these statements is correct?**

   A   It is a criminal offence to have a car without motor insurance

   B   It is not a criminal offence to have a car without motor
       insurance if you only drive it occasionally

20 **When might you need a CRB check?**

   A   When applying for welfare benefits

   B   When applying for work that involves children or vulnerable people

   C   When buying a house

   D   When requesting medical treatment from the NHS

21 **What information must an employer show on pay slips?**
Select two options from below

   A   Tax that has been deducted from your pay

   B   National Insurance contributions that have
       been deducted from your pay

   C   The number of days holiday entitlement that you have remaining

   D   The date that your contract started

22 At what age can men get a state pension?

    A 55 years old

    B 60 years old

    C 65 years old

    D 70 years old

23 British citizens require a work permit before they can work in any country that is a member of the European Economic Area. Is this statement true or false?

    A True

    B False

24 Select the correct statement

    A Children are free to work at any time of the day

    B It is illegal for a child to work before 7am or after 7pm

PRACTICE TEST 9

1 There are more women than men in Britain's population.
Is this statement true or false?

    A True

    B False

2 At what age do school children take their first national test in Wales?

    A 7

    B 9

    C 11

    D 14

3 Which of these statements is correct?

    A It is illegal to be drunk in public

    B It is illegal to be drunk anywhere

4 What is the distance from John O'Groats on the north coast of Scotland to Land's End in the south-west corner of England?

    A Approximately 1,100 miles (1,770 kilometres)

    B Approximately 1,310 miles (2,110 kilometres)

    C Approximately 500 miles (800 kilometres)

    D Approximately 870 miles (1,400 kilometres)

5 What is the name of the established church in Scotland?

    A The Anglican Church

    B The Church of England

    C The Episcopal Church

    D The Presbyterian Church

6 Which of these statements is correct?

    A Boxing Day and New Year are both public holidays

    B New Year is a public holiday and Boxing Day is not

7 When is Guy Fawkes Night?

A The evening of 15 October

B The evening of 25 September

C The evening of 30 May

D The evening of 5 November

8 Which of these statements is correct?

A The House of Commons is the more important of the two chambers in Parliament

B The House of Lords is the more important of the two chambers in Parliament

9 Where is the Prime Minister's official residence?

A 10 Downing Street

B 12 Downing Street

C Buckingham Palace

D Palace of Westminster

10 How is the Speaker of the House of Commons chosen?

A Appointed by the King or Queen

B Chosen by the Prime Minister

C Elected by fellow MPs

D Elected by the public

11 Where do local authorities get most of their funding from?

A Government taxation

B Issuing parking tickets

C Local council tax

D Lottery grants

12 What is the name of the official record of proceedings in Parliament?

A Hansard

B Parliament News

C The Recorder

D Westminster Hour

13 Who is the head of the Commonwealth?

A The Archbishop of Canterbury

B The British Prime Minister

C The Queen

D The Secretary of the Commonwealth

14 The UK is a member of the European Union but not of the Council of Europe. Is this statement true or false?

A True

B False

15 Why will you be asked to give a landlord a deposit at the beginning of your tenancy?

A To cover the cost of any damage to the property

B To pay for electricity supply at the property

C To pay for keys to the property

D To start a bank account

16 When will the British government adopt the euro as the UK's currency?

A 2010

B 2015

C Never

D When the British people vote for it in a referendum

17 Within what period of time must a baby be registered with the Registrar of Births, Marriages and Deaths?

A One week

B Six months

C Six weeks

D Twelve months

18 What is the role of the National Trust?

A Collect the TV licence

B Guarantee a pension for government employees

C Maintain and enhance the residence of the Prime Minister

D Preserve important buildings and countryside in the UK

19 How often are you required to take your vehicle for an MOT test if it is over three years old?

A Every five years

B Every two years

C Every year

D You only need an MOT test if the car has been involved in an accident

20 In Northern Ireland, it is legal to discriminate on grounds of religious belief or political opinion. Is this statement true or false?

A True

B False

21 How many weeks of paid holiday each year are employees over 16 normally entitled to?

A Five weeks

B Four weeks

C Three weeks

D Two weeks

22 Which of these statements is correct?

    A Employers have a legal duty to make sure the workplace is safe

    B Employees have no responsibility to work safely

**23 All women workers are entitled to maternity pay.
Is this statement true or false?**

    A True

    B False

**24 What is the maximum number of hours that a
child can work in any school week?**

    A 12 hours

    B 18 hours

    C 20 hours

    D 38 hours

PRACTICE TEST 10

1   There are more men in study at university than women.
    Is this statement true or false?

    A   True

    B   False

2   Which of these statements is correct?

    A   It is compulsory for children aged between 5 and 16 to attend school

    B   Children aged over 14 do not have to attend school

3   Which of these statements is correct?

    A   It is illegal to possess cannabis anywhere

    B   It is legal to possess cannabis in the privacy of your own home

4   Where is the Scouse dialect spoken?

    A   Cornwall

    B   Liverpool

    C   London

    D   Tyneside

5   The Church of England is called the Episcopal Church in Scotland.
    Is this statement true or false?

    A   True

    B   False

6   When is Boxing Day?

    A   1 January

    B   25 December

    C   26 December

    D   31 December

7   What does Guy Fawkes Night commemorate?

A   Remembrance of those killed during war

B   The failure of a plot to bomb Parliament

C   The invention of fireworks

D   The rebuilding of the Houses of Parliament

8   The Prime Minister and most members of the Cabinet are MPs. Is this statement true or false?

A   True

B   False

9   A Prime Minister can be removed from office by their party at any time. Is this statement true or false?

A   True

B   False

10   There are no independent MPs in Parliament. Is this statement true or false?

A   True

B   False

11   All candidates standing for office in local government must be members of a political party. Is this statement true or false?

A   True

B   False

12   Newspapers can not publish political opinions or run campaigns to influence government. Is this statement true or false?

A   True

B   False

13 How many member states are there in the Commonwealth?

A 25 member states

B 39 member states

C 53 member states

D 75 member states

14 What is the purpose of the Council of Europe?

A To create a single market for members of the council

B To create new European regulations and directives

C To debate proposals, decisions and expenditure of the European Commission

D To develop conventions which focus on human rights, democracy, education, the environment, health and culture

15 Choose the correct statement from below

A After a tenancy agreement has been signed, a landlord cannot raise the rent without agreement from the tenant

B A landlord can raise the rent, but only one month after the tenancy agreement has been signed

16 Who are welfare benefits not available to?

A The sick and disabled

B The elderly

C The unemployed

D People who do not have legal rights of residence in the UK

17 If a child does not attend school, that child's parent or guardian may be prosecuted. Is this statement true or false?

A True

B False

18 What is the minimum age to be able to drink alcohol in a pub?

A   16 years old

B   18 years old

C   21 years old

D   It depends if you are with an adult

19 What is the speed limit for cars and motorcycles in built-up areas?

A   30 miles per hour

B   50 miles per hour

C   60 miles per hour

D   70 miles per hour

20 By law, men and women who do the same job should receive equal pay. Is this statement true or false?

A   True

B   False

21 Select the correct statement from below

A   If you are self-employed then you need to pay your own tax

B   People that are self-employed have tax automatically taken from their earnings

22 Who should you speak to if you have health and safety concerns in your workplace? Select two answers from below

A   Your supervisor or manager

B   The police

C   Your local MP

D   Your trade union representative

23 Women are only entitled to maternity leave after they have completed their first year in a job. Is this statement true or false?

A   True

B   False

24 Select the correct statement

A Children are allowed to work for the full duration of their school holidays

B Children must have at least two consecutive weeks a year during their holidays where they do not work

FURTHER READING

Life in the UK Test: Practice Questions
ISBN 978-0955215933

An excellent revision aid for anyone wanting to check their knowledge of the study materials for the British citizenship or settlement tests. The second edition of this test book is packed with over 400 practice questions in the same format as those used in the official test, and has been revised to cover the new 2007 study materials published by the Home Office.

Citizens Advice Handbook: Practical, Independent Advice
ISBN 978-0141016788

A useful handbook brimming with information covering everything from employment to education and housing. This book is published by the Citizens Advice Bureau which is a registered charity providing free information and advice throughout the UK. Drawing on years of experience and a vast bank of resources, Citizens Advice is uniquely placed to give the most up-to-date information about the procedures and practices that affect everyone in the UK.

London Explorer: The Complete Residents' Guide
ISBN 978-9768182968

London Explorer is filled with invaluable information and advice for residents and expats living in this vibrant part of the world. Meticulously researched and written by residents who know the place inside out, it contains all the insider info anyone could need to help them make the most of living, working and playing in the city. With the most in-depth, practical and accurate coverage of London and its surrounding areas, the London Explorer is the ultimate companion for residents, whether they've just stepped off the plane or have been here for years.

Although you will not be asked questions about the other chapters of the book 'Life in the United Kingdom: A Journey to Citizenship', you may download them from our website. The chapters contain further information about British history, laws and organisations.

For further information visit **www.lifeintheuk.net/extras**

ANSWERS

Answers to Revision Questions

1 In the past immigrant groups came to invade and seize land. Now people come in search of jobs and a better life

2 Irish labourers provided much of the workforce to construct the canals and railways of the UK

3 Aid the reconstruction effort after the Second World War

4 Uganda and Vietnam

5 United States, Australia, South Africa and New Zealand

6 To escape religious persecution

7 West Indies

8 India and Pakistan

9 1857

10 Women over the age of 30 got the right to vote in 1918

11 45%

12 There are more women than men in university

13 1928

14 Three quarters of women in the UK, who have children, are in paid work

15 15 million

16 35% of children do not live with both birth parents
25% live in single parent families
10% live in stepfamilies

17 Most children in Britain receive weekly pocket money

18 65%

19 Two million

20 One in three move on to higher education

21 Tobacco must not be sold to anyone under the age of 18

22 One in five

23 59.8 million

24 Once every ten years

25 1801

26 Statistics about the population and topics such as age, place of birth, occupation, ethnicity, housing, health and marital status

27	2011
28	England, 50.1 million; Scotland, 5.1 million; Wales, 2.9 million; Northern Ireland, 1.7 million
29	100 years
30	People of Indian descent
31	About half
32	Ethnic minorities make up about 8% of UK population
33	45%
34	29%
35	About 870 miles (approximately 1,400 kilometres)
36	Highlands and Islands of Scotland
37	Wales
38	Tyneside
39	London
40	Liverpool
41	75%
42	Seven people out of ten stated their religion as Christian
43	2.7%
44	The Anglican Church
45	Supreme Governor
46	Anyone who is not Protestant
47	The King or Queen appoints the Archbishop of Canterbury after taking advice from the Prime Minister, which is based on a recommendation from a Church appointed committee
48	10%
49	St David's Day: Wales – 1 March St Patrick's Day: Northern Ireland – 17 March St George's Day: England – 23 April St Andrew's Day: Scotland – 30 November
50	St Patrick's Day in Northern Ireland
51	Football, tennis, rugby and cricket are very popular in the UK
52	Christmas Day is 25 December each year. Christmas celebrates the birth of Jesus Christ
53	A special meal that often includes turkey
54	1 January each year

55 Valentine's Day is observed on 14 February each year. On this day, couples exchange cards and gifts. Sometimes cards are sent anonymously

56 Mothering Sunday is held three weeks before Easter. On this day, people remember their mothers by giving gifts and flowers and trying to make their day as enjoyable as possible

57 April Fool's Day is celebrated on 1 April each year. On this day, people play jokes on each other, but only until noon

58 Guy Fawkes Night is held on the evening of 5 November each year. The night commemorates an event when a Catholic group plotted to bomb the Houses of Parliament and kill the King

59 Remembrance Day is observed on 11 November each year. It commemorates the memory of those who died during war

60 31 December each year

61 People wear artificial poppies in buttonholes in memory of those that lost their lives during war

62 The Prime Minister is the leader of the political party in power

63 At least once every five years

64 10 Downing Street in London

65 A committee of about 20 MPs, from the party that forms the Government, that meets to decide general policies for government

66 Chancellor of the Exchequer

67 Home Secretary

68 They are submitted to Parliament for debate or approval

69 Member of Parliament

70 About 20 MPs

71 The party with the most MPs elected into the House of Commons forms the Government

72 The Opposition

73 An unwritten constitution

74 To chair proceedings in the House of Commons

75 They are held to replace an MP when they resign or die while in office

76 The Queen

77 Represent their constituency; help create new laws; scrutinise and comment on what the government is doing; debate important national issues

78 The opening of parliament

79	The Speaker is elected to the position by fellow MPs
80	A small group of MPs that ensure discipline and attendance of MPs at voting time in the House of Commons
81	A member of the House of Lords who has been appointed by the Prime Minister – but only for the member's lifetime
82	Members of the House of Commons are democratically elected. They review, debate and vote on new laws or amendments. The House of Lords is made up of peers, who are not elected. They review new laws already passed by the House of Commons. They also propose new laws, which are then discussed by the House of Commons
83	The "first past the post" system
84	The candidate must win the most votes out of all candidates
85	Hansard
86	Non-departmental public bodies. They are independent agencies set up by the government
87	Tickets to the public galleries can be obtained from your local MP or by queueing on the day at the public entrance
88	Proportional representation is used in the Scottish Parliament, Welsh Assembly and Northern Ireland Assembly
89	Neutrality and professionalism regardless of the party in power
90	The police are organised locally, usually each county has its own police force
91	To provide community services in their local area, such as education, housing, social services, transport, fire services, rubbish collection, planning, environmental health and libraries
92	From central government taxation; only 20% of funding is provided through council tax
93	May each year
94	Full civic rights to vote in all elections and duties such as jury service
95	A candidate must be a citizen of the United Kingdom, Irish Republic or Commonwealth and be 18 years or over
96	By completing an electoral registration form. These forms are sent to households in September and October each year
97	The European Commission is the civil service of the EU. It drafts proposals for new EU policies and laws. It also administers EU funding programmes

98 To draw up conventions which focus on human rights, democracy, education, the environment, health and culture

99 1973

100 For member states to become a single market

101 A group within the EU made up of government ministers from each member state. It passes new EU laws and takes the most important decisions about how the EU is run

102 Brussels

103 To examine and debate the proposals, decisions and expenditure of the European Council and European Commission

104 Subject to some restrictions, citizens of an EU member state have the right to travel to and work in any EU country if they have a valid passport or identity card

105 53 member states

106 An international organisation that works to prevent war and maintain peace and security

107 It is a permanent member of the UN Security Council

108 Estate agents represent the person selling a house or flat. They arrange for buyers to visit homes that are for sale

109 If you are homeless you can get help from your local authority (or, in Northern Ireland, the Housing Executive)

110 Carries out checks on the home that you want to buy

111 Two thirds

112 Put your name on the council register or list

113 To cover the cost of any damage that occurs during the tenancy

114 Council Tax funds many local government services, such as education, police, roads, refuse collection and libraries

115 Try speaking to them first. If you cannot resolve the problems, speak to your landlord, local authority or housing association

116 Either according to the size of the home or using a water meter

117 The local authority

118 Fire, theft and accidental damage

119 You need to show documents to prove your identity, such as a passport, immigration document or driving licence. You also need to show something with your address on it like a tenancy agreement or household bill

120 All of these cards allow you to pay for things without using cash. However, to use a debit card you must have enough money in your bank account to cover the cost of what you buy. Credit and store cards do not draw money from your bank account, but you are sent a bill that you must pay every month. Store cards can only be used in a specific shop

121 Credit unions are financial co-operatives owned and controlled by their members. The members pool their savings and then make loans from this pool

122 Guides to benefits are available from Jobcentre Plus offices, local libraries, post offices and the Citizens Advice Bureau

123 If you have debt problems you should speak to your bank or building society as soon as you can. You should also get advice from the Citizens Advice Bureau

124 £5, £10, £20 and £50 notes

125 Visit your local health centre, or surgery, to find out what you need to do to register. Usually you must have a medical card. If you do not have one, the GP's receptionist should give you a form to send to the local health authority. They will then send you a medical card

126 You can get the name of a dentist by asking at the local library, at the Citizens Advice Bureau and through NHS Direct

127 When you require emergency medical treatment

128 For emergency calls for police, fire or ambulance services

129 Provides telephone advice on particular health conditions

130 You will can receive care from your local hospital, local health centre or from special ante-natal clinics. You will receive support from a GP and from a midwife

131 Registrar of Births, Marriages and Deaths (Register Office) within six weeks of the birth

132 In most parts of the UK, compulsory education is divided into two stages, primary and secondary. In England and Wales the primary stage lasts from 5 to 11, in Scotland from 5 to 12 and in Northern Ireland from 4 to 11. The secondary stage lasts until the age of 16. At that age young people can choose to leave school or to continue with their secondary education until they are 17 or 18

133 Education at state schools in the UK is provided by the government and is free. Faith schools are linked to a religion or church. Integrated schools aim to bring children of different religions together. Independent schools are private schools that are not run or paid for by the state. At independent schools parents must pay the full cost of their child's education

134 The subjects required by the government to be taught in schools. This includes English, maths, science, design and technology, information and communication technology (ICT), history, geography, modern foreign languages, art and design, music, physical education (PE) and citizenship

135 The governing body decides how the school is run and administered and produces reports on the progress of the school from year to year. A number of places on a school's governing body are reserved for parents

136 Courses are available for people wishing to improve their skills in English (known as ESOL or English for Speakers of Other Languages); literacy and numeracy courses. Plus courses to learn new skills for employment

137 Films are classified using the following rating system:
U (Universal): Suitable for anyone aged 4 years and over;
PG (parental guidance): Suitable for everyone but some parts of the film might be unsuitable for children. Their parents should decide;
12 or 12a: Children under 12 are not allowed to see or rent the film unless they are with an adult;
15: Children under 15 are not allowed to see or rent the film;
18: No one under 18 is allowed to see or rent the film;
R18: No one under 18 is allowed to see the film, which is only available in specially licensed cinemas

138 Anyone in the UK with a television (TV), DVD or video recorder, computer or any device which is used for watching or recording TV programmes must buy a television licence

139 To buy or drink alcohol you must be 18 or over. The landlord of a pub may allow people of 14 to come into the pub but they are not allowed to drink. At 16, people can drink wine or beer with a meal in a hotel or restaurant

140 A charity that works to preserve important buildings and countryside

141 Once you have reached the required driving age you can apply for a provisional licence. You then need to pass a written theory test and a practical driving test

142 You must have either a valid driving licence issued in the UK or EU (including Iceland, Liechtenstein or Norway), or if you have a licence from a country outside the EU, you may use it in the UK for up to 12 months

143 Don't drive away without stopping – this is a criminal offence.
Call the police and ambulance on 999 or 112 if someone is injured.
Get the names, addresses, vehicle registration numbers and insurance details
of the other drivers.
Give your details to the other drivers or passengers and to the police.
Make a note of everything that happened and contact your insurance
company as soon as possible

144 You may have to prove your identity at different times, such as when you
open a bank account, rent accommodation, enrol for a college course, hire
a car, apply for benefits such as housing benefit, or apply for a marriage
certificate

145 There are many different ways of proving your identity - these include:
- Official documents from the Home Office showing your immigration status
- A certificate of identity
- A passport or travel document
- A National Insurance (NI) number card
- A provisional or full driving licence
- A recent gas, electricity or phone bill showing your name and address
- A rent or benefits book

146 30 mph in built up areas; 60 mph on single carriageways; 70 mph on dual
carriageways

147 The Home Office provides guidance on who is allowed to work in the UK. Not
everyone in the UK is allowed to work and some people need work permits

148 By contacting the National Academic Recognition Information Centre (NARIC)

149 A document that gives specific details on your education, qualifications,
previous employment, skills and interests

150 Referees are people that know you well and agree to write a short report or
reference on your suitability for a job. Personal friends or members of your
family are not normally acceptable as referees

151 If an employer later finds out that you gave incorrect information, you might
lose your job

152 If you apply for work that involves working with children or vulnerable people

153 Jobcentre Plus lists vacancies and training opportunities

154 Voluntary work can be a good way to support and get involved in your local
community. It also provides useful work experience that can help with future
job applications

55 It is against the law for employers to discriminate against someone at work because of their:
- Sex
- Nationality, race, colour or ethnic group
- Disability
- Religion
- Sexual orientation
- Age

In Northern Ireland, the law also bans discrimination on grounds of religious belief or political opinion. However, discrimination is not against the law when the job involves working for someone in their own home

156 The law states that men and women who do the same job, or work of equal value, should receive equal pay

157 The Commission for Racial Equality can help with racial discrimination. The Equal Opportunities Commission can help with sex discrimination issues. The Disability Rights Commission deals with disability issues. From October 2007 all these groups will be brought together in the new Commission for Equality and Human Rights

158 • Indecent remarks or comments about the way you look that make you feel uncomfortable or humiliated
- Comments or questions about your sex life
- Inappropriate touching or sexual demands
- Bullying behaviour or being treated in a way that is rude, hostile, degrading or humiliating because of your sex

159 The contract or written statement is important and useful if there is ever a disagreement about your work, pay or conditions

160 For workers aged 22 and above £5.35 an hour
For 18–21 year olds £4.45 an hour
For 16-17 year olds £3.30 an hour

161 Pay slips must show exactly how much money has been taken off for tax and National Insurance contributions

162 Trade unions are organisations that aim to improve the pay and working conditions of their members

163 If you have problems of any kind at work, speak to your supervisor, manager, trade union representative or someone else with responsibility as soon as possible. If you need advice and are a member of a trade union, your representative will help. You can also contact your local Citizens Advice Bureau or Law Centre

164 For serious misconduct at work.
If after receiving a warning, your work, punctuality or attendance does not improve

165 A court which specialises in employment matters

166 You can ask for advice and information on your legal rights and the best action to take from your trade union representative, a solicitor, a Law Centre or the Citizens Advice Bureau

167 You normally only have three months to make a complaint if you want to take your case to an Employment Tribunal

168 If you lose your job because the company you work for no longer needs you to do your job, or can no longer afford to employ you

169 For most people, income tax and National Insurance contributions are automatically taken from their earnings. Money raised from income tax pays for government services such as roads, education, police and the armed forces

170 If you are employed then tax is automatically taken from your earnings by your employer and paid directly to HM Revenue and Customs.
If you are self-employed then you need to pay your own tax

171 You can get help and advice from the HM Revenue and Customs self-assessment helpline

172 Anyone who does not pay enough NI contributions will not be able to receive certain benefits, such as Jobseeker's Allowance or Maternity Pay, and may not receive a full state retirement pension

173 Applications can be made at Jobcentre Plus or your local Social Security Office

174 Everyone in the UK who has paid enough National Insurance contributions will get a state pension when they retire

175 The state pension age for men is currently 65 years of age and for women it is 60

176 Employers have a legal duty to make sure the workplace is safe. Employees also have a legal duty to follow safety regulations and to work safely and responsibly

177 If you are worried about health and safety at your workplace, talk to your supervisor, manager or trade union representative

178 If you are self-employed then you have a responsibility to keep detailed records and to pay your own tax and National Insurance

179 Business Link is a government funded project that provides advice for people starting or running a business

180 It is important to follow the correct procedures and to give notice to your employer well in advance before taking leave

181 13 years old (there are exceptions for some types of performance work)

182 They can only do light work. Children under 16 are not allowed to do jobs such as delivering milk, selling alcohol, cigarettes or medicines, working in a kitchen or behind the counter of a chip shop, working with dangerous machinery or chemicals, or doing any other kind of work that may be harmful to their health or education.

183 12 hours a week

184 Any child under 16 seeking to do paid work must apply for a licence from the local authority. Children taking part in some kinds of performances may have to obtain a medical certificate before working

185 Parents must ensure their child works within the law and receives a proper education

HOW TO USE THE MARKING SHEET

Tear out or photocopy this marking sheet to make it easier to record and check your answers.

Each row can be easily matched up with the answers printed on page 205

You can also download and print out a copy of this marking sheet from our website by visiting www.lifeintheuk.net/marking-sheet

MARKING SHEET

	Test 1	Test 2	Test 3	Test 4	Test 5	Test 6	Test 7	Test 8	Test 9	Test 10
1										
2										
3										
4										
5										
6										
7										
8										
9										
10										
11										
12										
13										
14										
15										
16										
17										
18										
19										
20										
21										
22										
23										
24										
Total										

SCORING GUIDE

Check your test results using this scoring guide.

Less than 6	**Very poor** – Do not take any further practice tests until significant revision has been completed.
7–12	**Unsatisfactory** – Considerable gaps in knowledge. Further revision of study materials required.
13–17	**Good** – Not quite ready yet. Revise your weak areas to complete your knowledge.
18 or more	**Excellent** – Well done! You are above the pass mark and are now ready to sit the official test.

PRACTICE TEST ANSWERS

	Test 1	Test 2	Test 3	Test 4	Test 5	Test 6	Test 7	Test 8	Test 9	Test 10
1	D	D	C	A	D	B	D	C	A	B
2	B	B	C	B	C	C	A	B	D	A
3	B	B	D	C	A	B	B	C & D	A	A
4	C	A	C	C	B	D	C	C	D	B
5	C	D	B	D	A	D	C	D	D	A
6	A	B	C	D	D	A	B	A	A	C
7	A	D	C	C	A	C	D	B	D	B
8	B	D	C	D	D	B	B	C	A	A
9	D	C	B	C	A & B	B	A	A & B	A	A
10	C	D	B	D	C	D	C	A & B	C	B
11	A	A & B	D	D	A	A & D	A & D	B	A	B
12	C	D	B	C	C	B	B	B	A	B
13	B	A & B	B	B	B	A & B	A	A	C	C
14	C	C	B	A	A	A	C	A	B	D
15	A & B	B	B	C	A	A	A	A	A	A
16	C	A	A & B	A & B	B	A & B	D	B	D	D
17	C & D	A	B	A	A	A	A	A & B	C	A
18	C	B	D	C	B	D	C	A	D	B
19	B	D	B	A	A & C	B	A	A	C	A
20	D	A	B	A	B	B	A & D	B	B	A
21	B	D	B	A	C	A	B	A & B	B	A
22	A	A & B	A & B	B	D	A & B	B	C	A	A & D
23	B	B	A	A & B	B	C	A	B	B	B
24	B	B	D	B	C	C	B	B	A	B

USEFUL PHONE NUMBERS

The phone numbers below may be useful in finding more information about the Life in the UK Test, applications for settlement or citizenship and accessing services discussed in the study materials.

Life in the UK Test Helpline 0800 0154245

Call for all enquiries relating to the Life in the UK Test

Border & Immigration Agency: Immigration Enquiry Bureau 0870 6067766

Call for enquiries relating to settlement or indefinite leave to remain

Border & Immigration Agency: Nationality Enquiries 0845 0105200

Call for enquiries relating to citizenship and nationality

Identity and Passport Service: Passport Advice Line 0870 5210410

Call for enquiries relating to the issue of passports

Learndirect 0800 100900

Call for information on further education including courses for English for speakers of other languages (ESOL)

UPDATE TO STUDY MATERIALS

Many of the facts that you need to learn for your test relate to laws and regulations determined and administered by the government. The study materials in this book were published by the Home Office in February 2007. Since that time some laws and regulations have changed, meaning that some facts in this book are out of date.

However, the Home Office advises that your test will ONLY cover published material. You are NOT required to know that a law or regulation has changed.

While these changes to laws and regulations will not be reflected in your test you may be interested to know what they are. An updated list of the changes can be found on our website by visiting **www.lifeintheuk.net/out-of-date**

CD ROM INSTRUCTIONS

This CD ROM contains software that lets you take further practice tests using your PC. You can also enable feedback after each question which will direct you to the relevant page in the study guide for questions you get wrong.

The software on this CD ROM requires the following:

- Microsoft® Windows® 2000, XP or Vista

- 256 MB of installed RAM

- 533 Mhz Processor or better

- 10 MB Hard Drive Space

Installation

Use the following instructions to install the study guide software on your PC.

1. Restart Windows and turn off any antivirus software.

2. Insert the CD ROM. Your computer should automatically load the installation programme. Alternatively, you may start the installation programme by running the **start.exe** file located on the CD ROM.

3. When the CD install menu appears, click on the Install Software button.

4. When the setup wizard screen appears, click *Next*. Follow the on-screen instructions to review and accept the License Agreement.

5. Click *Next*, and follow the on-screen instructions to start the installation. If the installation was successful then click *Finish*.

You can start the study guide software by double-clicking the shortcut on the desktop or by clicking on the Life in the UK Test Study Guide CD icon in the Start menu.

For late-breaking information about issues related to installation, visit **www.lifeintheuk.net/cdhelp**

VISIT

www.lifeintheuk.net

for the latest news and advice about the test
